THE 2018 CHELTENHAM FESTIVAL STALLION GUIDE

Welcome to the fourth edition of the

Cheltenham Festival Stallion Gui(

Introduction from the Author – James Iddiols

When it comes to the Cheltenham Festival, there is compelling evidence that a horse's breeding is a critical factor when it comes to picking winners. The progeny of some stallions perform creditably at the festival time and time again, whereas others consistently struggle. For example, one would have made a profit at every festival meeting from 2013 – 2017, had one blindly bet at level stakes on every single **Milan** sired festival entry. One would have also made a profit for those five years adopting exactly the same approach on **Shantou**'s progeny. On the other hand, if one wants to throw money away, the best stallion to follow is **Definite Article**.

This Guide analyses each sire's festival record based upon the performance and results of that sire's offspring over the past ten festivals. The result is an analysis and commentary on 40 stallions upon which there is evidence of a statistical trend and where the progeny are likely to be represented at the 2018 Cheltenham Festival. Armed with the Guide's clear-sighted information and recommendations, punters have a new angle on which to make their betting selections and hopefully improve their chances of beating the bookmakers.

My aim is not only to provide an analysis on each stallion that is easy to follow and insightful for betting purposes, but I also hope to successfully re-ignite fond memories for Cheltenham Festival devotees by highlighting previous races and runners together with some fascinating observations and thought-provoking festival trivia.

Looking back at last year's meeting, it was back to normal in terms of witnessing some surprises and a few big outsiders coming in. In contrast, the 2016 Cheltenham Festival was somewhat unusual with eleven winning favourites and only one 20/1 plus winner. ***Labaik*** set the tone of the 2017 Cheltenham Festival when causing a surprise in the opening *Sky Bet Supreme Novices' Hurdle*, winning at a price of 25/1. He all but refused to start on his previous three outings. The following day, we were in for another shock when 2/9 odds on favourite ***Douvan*** flopped in the *Betway Queen Mother Champion Chase*. And who would have thought that trainer *Willie Mullins* would be winless after the first two days of last year's festival, although he made up for it on the Thursday and Friday, picking up 6 of the 14 races that remained.

One of the most memorable performances for me at last year's festival was ***Un De Sceaux***'s domineering performance in the *Ryanair Chase* under what was a superb ride by *Ruby Walsh*. But, my favourite race was the *Weatherbys Champion Bumper* where ***Fayonagh*** came from the back before sprinting past the entire field to win. Sadly the mare was put down in October last year following an injury on the gallops. You can read about her win and why she is on the front cover of this Guide in the chapter on her sire, **Kalanisi**.

With regard to the analysis and advice provided within the Stallion Guide last year, for the most part, the recommendations were accurate. The results from last year supported my positive views about runners sired by **Authorized**, **Midnight Legend**, **Milan**, **Old Vic**, **Poliglote**, **Saddler Maker**, **Shantou** and **Stowaway**, as well as my negative opinion about the chances of those entries sired by **Al Namix**, **Beneficial**, **Definite Article** and **Kapgarde**. The two stallions whose stock disappointed at the 2017 Cheltenham Festival were **Gold Well** and **Westerner**.

The 2018 Cheltenham Festival Stallion Guide features four "new entries", generally younger stallions whose offspring have started to provide some early positive or negative festival trends. The sires making their debut appearance in this year's Guide are **Califet, Martaline, Network and Vinnie Roe.** I have also dropped eight stallions from the Guide, either because the sire is not producing the quality of offspring rated high enough to get a run at the festival or simply due to the fact that the stallion's progeny are now too old to race. The eight who have appeared in previous Stallion Guides, but are not featured in 2018 are **Alflora, Assessor, Fragrant Mix, Hernando, Heron Island, Karinga Bay, Sir Harry Lewis** and **Turtle Island.**

In this year's Guide, I have included the 2018 Cheltenham Festival race schedule and alongside each event, for reference purposes, the race format and distance. I hope readers find it a useful addition. Also, as was introduced in 2017, at the back of this Guide, there is a table of the stallions featured in the Guide along with a list of their offspring that, as of January 2017, were showing an official rating of 130 or greater.

Readers may be interested to know that the 40 stallions listed in this 2018 Cheltenham Festival Stallion Guide produced exactly 14 of last year's 28 winners. 488 horses took part at the 2017 Cheltenham Festival, of which 53%, or 261 runners, were sired by stallions featured in this year's Guide. For the record, a total of 713 stallions have been responsible for the 4,792 entries to have run at the festival in the past decade, and of those, 16.5% have had ten or more festival runners.

I hope you enjoy reading this year's Stallion Guide and if you have any views or comments, please feel free to contact me on Twitter @festivalsires. I wish you all an enjoyable and rewarding 2018 Cheltenham Festival.

James Iddiols @festivalsires

Highlights from the 2017 Cheltenham Festival Stallion Guide

Quotes from the 2017Cheltenham Festival Stallion Guide	What happened at the festival?
"The cut-off point for whether an **Authorized** bred festival runner is worth supporting or not, is a starting price of 16/1"	Two of the six **Authorized** bred entries came home winners. ***Tiger Roll*** at 16/1 and ***Nichols Canyon*** at 10/1.
"If you come across a horse that has **Midnight Legend** listed as the sire, then put your each-way bet on. The trends suggest that for one in every four bets, you can collect some winnings."	A victory and two places from eight festival appearances, the highlight being ***Sizing John***'s *Gold Cup* triumph.
"Over the past three festivals, **Milan** bred runners have recorded a win or place from close to one in every three runs."	4 of the 13 of **Milan**'s offspring that took part at the festival were placed.
"The *Fulke Walwyn Kim Muir Challenge Cup Handicap Chase* has been a strikingly rewarding race for **Old Vic** supporters over the past five years, where the progeny have a 100% record of securing a win or place dividend."	The **Old Vic** sired ***Pendra*** finished runner-up in the Kim Muir at 16/1.
"Come the 2017 Cheltenham Festival, it is a given that **Poliglote**'s progeny should be treated with the utmost respect."	All four **Poliglote** bred runners that appeared at the 2017 Cheltenham Festival secured a top four finishing position
"The data is beyond question. Punters will make a profit betting on **Shantou**'s offspring at Cheltenham Festivals."	Blindly backing every **Shantou** bred runner at level stakes resulted in a profit for the fifth successive Cheltenham Festival.
"Punters should take a serious interest if they find any **Sinndar** bred runners among the list of entries in Wednesday's *Fred Winter Juvenile Novices' Handicap Hurdle*."	The **Sinndar** sired ***Project Bluebook***, rewarded each-way backers by securing 4th place in the *Fred Winter* at 14/1.
"My hunch is that, over time, **Stowaway**'s progeny will provide us with further festival successes."	From 4 representatives, **Stowaway**'s offspring delivered a 12/1 victory, a 9/1 place and another runner who looked likely to be in the shake up before falling.

Cheltenham Festival 2018 – Race Schedule *(as of 31st December 2017)*

Tuesday 13th March 2018	*Hurdles*			*Chases*				*Bumper*
	2m	*2½m*	*3m*	*2m*	*2½m*	*3m*	*4m*	*2m*
1.30pm *The Sky Bet Supreme Novices' Hurdle Race*	✓							
2.10pm *The Racing Post Arkle Challenge Trophy Steeple Chase*				✓				
2.50pm *The Ultima Handicap Steeple Chase*						✓		
3.30pm *The Unibet Champion Hurdle Challenge Trophy*	✓							
4.10pm *The OLBG Mares' Hurdle Race*		✓						
4.50pm *The National Hunt (Amateur Riders' Novices' Steeple Chase) Challenge Cup*							✓	
5.30pm *The Close Brothers Novices' Handicap Chase*					✓			

Wednesday 14th March 2018	*Hurdles*			*Chases*				*Bumper*
	2m	*2½m*	*3m*	*2m*	*2½m*	*3m*	*4m*	*2m*
1.30pm *The Ballymore Novices' Hurdle Race*		✓						
2.10pm *The RSA Steeple Chase*						✓		
2.50pm *The Coral Cup Hurdle (A Handicap Hurdle Race)*		✓						
3.30pm *The Betway Queen Mother Champion Steeple Chase*				✓				
4.10pm *The Glenfarclas Cross Country Steeple Chase*							✓	
4.50pm *The Boodles Fred Winter Juvenile Handicap Hurdle Race*	✓							
5.30pm *The Weatherbys Champion Bumper (A Standard Open NH Flat Race)*								✓

Thursday 15th March 2018	*Hurdles*			*Chases*				*Bumper*
	2m	*2½m*	*3m*	*2m*	*2½m*	*3m*	*4m*	*2m*
1.30pm *The JLT Novices' Chase*					✓			
2.10pm *The Pertemps Network Final (A Handicap Hurdle Race)*			✓					
2.50pm *The Ryanair Steeple Chase*					✓			
3.30pm *The Sun Bets Stayers' Hurdle*			✓					
4.10pm *The Brown Advisory & Merriebelle Stable Plate (A Handicap Steeple Chase)*					✓			
4.50pm *The Trull House Stud Mares Novices' Hurdle*	✓							
5.30pm *The Fulke Walwyn Kim Muir Challenge Cup Handicap Steeple Chase*						✓		

Friday 16th March 2018	*Hurdles*			*Chases*				*Bumper*
	2m	*2½m*	*3m*	*2m*	*2½m*	*3m*	*4m*	*2m*
1.30pm *The JCB Triumph Hurdle*	✓							
2.10pm *The Randox Health County Handicap Hurdle Race*	✓							
2.50pm *The Albert Bartlett Novices' Hurdle Race*			✓					
3.30pm *The Timico Cheltenham Gold Cup Steeple Chase*						✓		
4.10pm *The St. James's Place Foxhunter Steeple Chase Challenge Cup*						✓		
4.50pm *The Martin Pipe Conditional Jockeys' Handicap Hurdle Race*		✓						
5.30pm *The Johnny Henderson Grand Annual Handicap Steeple Chase Challenge Cup*				✓				

Right hand columns show race categories (by race format and nearest distance to a half mile)

Contents

Stallions

Al Namix (FR)

Quote from the 2017 Cheltenham Festival Stallion Guide - "The progeny of **Al Namix** have so far flattered to deceive. And until the offspring start to deliver festival performances more in keeping with what the market would have us believe, then I will not be placing any wagers on **Al Namix** bred entries at the 2017 Cheltenham Festival."

Al Namix (21-y-o)							
Race Format	*Miles*	*Won*	*Placed*	*Unplaced*	*Total*	*Win %*	*Place %*
Hurdles	About 2m	0	2	7	9	0%	22%
	About 2m 4f	0	0	6	6	0%	0%
	About 3m	0	1	2	3	0%	33%
Chases	About 2m	0	0	1	1	0%	0%
	About 2m 4f	0	0	1	1	0%	0%
	About 3m	0	0	2	2	0%	0%
	About 4m	0	0	1	1	0%	0%
Bumper	About 2m	0	0	0	0	-	-
Total	**2008-2017**	**0**	**3**	**20**	**23**	**0%**	**13%**

It is still early days, but based on the twelve of **Al Namix**'s offspring who combined together have raced a total of 23 times at the Cheltenham Festival, it would appear that the progeny aren't at their best in early spring, racing on a left handed course with undulations, where the atmosphere is electric. With zero wins and just three places from 23 festival appearances, it seems unlikely that **Al Namix** will go down in the record books as a stallion prolific in producing festival winners.

Sometimes, there are some mitigating circumstances for a stallion's poor festival record, very often the reason being that the vast majority of the sire's runners are big priced outsiders, but that isn't the case with **Al Namix**. Just over a third of **Al Namix** bred runners lined up in their festival races within a narrow price range between 9/2 and 7/1 with three of them being sent off as the favourite. A further six runners were priced up between 9/1 and 20/1.

Six of the offspring have run at the Cheltenham Festival more than once, of which three have been successful in securing a place dividend. The *Nicky Henderson* trained, ***Grandouet***, has been to the festival on three occasions, his first run being in the 2011 *JCB Triumph Hurdle*, where he finished 3rd at a price of 13/2. Two years later in 2013, ***Grandouet*** was a faller in the *Stan James Champion Hurdle Challenge Trophy* and then registered a 6th placing over fences in the 2014 *Racing Post Arkle Challenge Trophy Chase*.

Saphir Du Rheu was having his fourth festival appearance at last year's meeting when finishing a very respectable 5th in the *Timico Cheltenham Gold Cup Chase* at a price of 33/1. His festival debut took place in 2013, when he was one of the 6/1 joint favourites for the *Fred Winter Juvenile Handicap Hurdle*, but he ran very disappointingly to finish 20th of 24 runners. Having missed the 2014 Cheltenham Festival, he returned two years later, this time as the outright 5/1 favourite, in the 2015 *Ladbrokes World Hurdle*. Although it was a much better performance from ***Saphir Du Rheu*** to finish as the runner-up, he came up against a rival who was having one of his best ever race days in the shape of 14/1 shot, *Cole Harden*, who made all and stayed on strongly up the Cheltenham Hill to win by 3¼ lengths. The following season, ***Saphir Du Rheu*** performed nowhere near as well he had in the

2016 running of the *World Hurdle* and ended up in sixth place some 40 lengths and more behind the very impressive winner, *Thistlecrack*.

Of the six runs from **Al Namix**'s progeny at last year's Cheltenham festival, the best performance was provided by ***Petit Mouchoir*** who was enjoying his second visit to the festival when leading from the front in the *Stan James Champion Hurdle Challenge Trophy*. It was a bold front-running performance from the 6 year-old, but once he was challenged two out, his early exertions caught up with him and he was unable to run on strongly up the run-in having to settle for third place at a price of 6/1. In his first festival appearance, ***Petit Mouchoir*** had finished 8th in the 2016 *Sky Bet Supreme Novices' Hurdle*.

Perhaps, in future, there will be an improvement in the festival performances and results of **Al Namix**'s progeny, but with a current state of play of just three placings and a loss of £39.50 had one placed a £1.00 each-way bet on all 23 appearances from the offspring, today's recommendation must be to ignore **Al Namix** sired runners at the 2018 Cheltenham Festival.

Astarabad (USA)

Quote from the 2017 Cheltenham Festival Stallion Guide - "The four **Astarabad** sired 4 year olds to have run at the festival, were all entered in the *Fred Winter Juvenile Novices' Handicap Hurdle* and all four secured at least a place."

Astarabad (Died as a 22-y-o in 2016)							
Race Format	*Miles*	*Won*	*Placed*	*Unplaced*	*Total*	*Win %*	*Place %*
Hurdles	About 2m	0	2	4	6	0%	33%
	About 2m 4f	1	0	6	7	14%	14%
	About 3m	0	0	3	3	0%	0%
Chases	About 2m	0	0	1	1	0%	0%
	About 2m 4f	0	0	2	2	0%	0%
	About 3m	0	1	0	1	0%	100%
	About 4m	0	0	0	0	-	-
Bumper	About 2m	1	0	0	1	100%	100%
Total	**2008-2017**	**2**	**3**	**16**	**21**	**10%**	**24%**

In total, 11 of **Astarabad**'s progeny have registered 23 festival appearances, 21 of which have taken place within the past decade. It was eleven years ago when the first two **Astarabad** sired horses appeared at a Cheltenham Festival, and both of them took part in the 2007 *Fred Winter Juvenile Novices' Handicap Hurdle*. ***Gaspara*** and ***Laustra Bad*** were both trained by *David Pipe* and it was a flying start for **Astarabad**, as ***Gaspara*** won the race with ***Laustra Bad*** some six lengths further back in third. ***Gaspara*** was the only filly in the race and her connections were delighted to not only win the *Fred Winter*, but also to pick up a £75,000 bonus, ***Gaspara*** having landed the *Sunderlands Imperial Cup Handicap Hurdle* at *Sandown* just three days earlier. If we add this race into the figures shown in the above table, from 23 runs in total, **Astarabad**'s offspring have delivered three wins and four place positions, which equates to a win and place strike rate of 30%.

Without doubt, the most lucrative event for **Astarabad**'s offspring is the *Fred Winter Juvenile Handicap Hurdle*. All four **Astarabad** sired 4 year olds to have run at the festival have been entered in this contest and all four have secured at least a place position. As highlighted above, in the 2007 running, the filly ***Gaspara*** was victorious at 9/2 with stablemate, ***Laustra Bad*** taking 3rd position at a price of 16/1. In 2008, the **Astarabad** sired ***Grand Schlem***, trained by French trainer, *Francois Doumen*, attempted to follow up ***Gaspara***'s success in the contest. Despite being up with the leaders and well in touch, ***Grand Schlem*** was a little one paced and eventually finished in third, at odds of 12/1. Eight years would pass before we would witness the 4th of **Astarabad**'s four year olds to race in the *Fred Winter*. In the 2016 contest, it was another mare, ***Missy Tata***, ridden by *Bryan Cooper* and trained by *Gordon Elliott*, who managed to take the fourth place dividend at odds of 10/1.

Gaspara, ***Cheltenian*** and ***Whisper*** are the three **Astarabad** sired horses that have provided this stallion's three festival victories. Interestingly, they are the only ones amongst **Astarabad**'s stock to have raced more than twice at a Cheltenham Festival. ***Gaspara*** and ***Whisper*** have competed in four events and ***Cheltenian*** has made five appearances. All three of them recorded their victories on their festival debuts.

Starting with ***Gaspara***, following her 2007 debut victory, at the next two festivals, she ran in the *David Nicholson Mares Hurdle*, finishing just outside the place positions on both occasions. Having finished 5th in the 2009 running of this mares race on the Tuesday, *David Pipe* entered her to run just three days later in the *Martin Pipe Conditional Jockeys' Handicap Hurdle*, where ***Gaspara*** was leading all the way to the second flight, at which point she unseated her rider!

Cheltenian opened his festival career with victory in the 2011 *Weatherbys Champion Bumper* at odds of 14/1. After missing the 2012 festival due to a tendon injury, ***Cheltenian*** returned to Cheltenham to compete in 2m hurdle events in successive years between 2013 and 2016. All four of these runs, however, were disappointing with 8th being the highest position attained, meaning that ***Cheltenian*** is the sole culprit for all four unplaced efforts showing in the above table's 2m hurdle category. After his 15th placing in the 2016 *Vincent O'Brien County Handicap Hurdle*, ***Cheltenian*** then headed up to *Haydock* for what was to be his last ever appearance on a racecourse. Sadly, on 7th May 2016, in the Grade 3 *Swinton Hurdle*, ***Cheltenian*** was quickly pulled up after suffering a fatal injury.

Whisper's debut win was achieved in the 2014 *Coral Cup*. It was an unforgettable day for ***Whisper***'s jockey *Nico de Boinville*, who secured his first ever festival victory riding his mount to win the race by a short head from *Get Me Out Of Here*, ridden by champion jockey, *A P McCoy*. Trainer *Nicky Henderson* entered ***Whisper*** in the *World Hurdle* for the next two festivals where he finished 5th in 2015 and 8th in 2016. At the 2017 Cheltenham Festival, ***Whisper*** participated in his 4th Cheltenham Festival when he lined up in the *RSA Novices' Chase*. It turned out to be a dramatic finish as ***Whisper***'s stablemate, ***Might Bite***, looked to have thrown the race away after the last when hanging dramatically to the stands' side. However, as ***Whisper*** rallied past, ***Might Bite*** ran on again in the final 100 yards to lead in the final stride and win by a nose. Having secured the runner-up spot, ***Whisper*** surpassed the achievements of ***Gaspara*** and ***Cheltenian*** who both failed to register a top three finishing position following their debut wins. There was only one other **Astarabad** representative at last year's festival, the *Gary Moore* trained ***Traffic Fluide***, who considering he was a 50/1 outsider, ran a very respectable race to finish 6th in the *Betway Queen Mother Champion Chase*.

At the time of writing, both ***Traffic Fluide*** and ***Whisper*** hold entries for the 2018 Cheltenham Festival. ***Traffic Fluide*** has an entry in the *Ryanair Chase* and if he makes the line-up, he will undoubtedly be a big priced outsider. If you fancy a flutter, be aware that in the thirteen years that the *Ryanair* has been in existence, only twice has the winner's starting price been bigger than 6/1; *Albertas Run* at 14/1 in 2010 and *Uxizandre* at 16/1 in 2015. ***Whisper*** has an entry in the 2018 *Timico Cheltenham Gold Cup Chase* and as for his chances, personally, I can't see him winning. ***Whisper*** is now ten years old which, perhaps surprisingly, is a big negative for winning the *Cheltenham Gold Cup*. Despite the fact that there have been a lot of short priced runners amongst them, 67 horses aged 10 or older have run in the *Gold Cup* this century. All have been beaten.

I won't be supporting either ***Traffic Fluide*** or ***Whisper*** should they line up at the festival this March. I will, however, be very interested should an **Astarabad** sired four year old be amongst the entries in the *Boodles Fred Winter Juvenile Handicap Hurdle*. To date, in four races in this contest, the progeny have a 100% record of providing punters with a return.

Authorized (IRE)

Quote from the 2017 Cheltenham Festival Stallion Guide - "Based on the 14 runs from the progeny to date, there is a pattern showing that the more fancied of **Authorized**'s stock are performing well at Cheltenham Festivals, whilst the outsiders are finishing well down the field in their races and performing to market expectations. As a guideline, the cut-off point for whether an **Authorized** bred festival runner is worth supporting or not, is a starting price of 16/1."

Authorized (14-y-o)								
Race Format	*Miles*	*Won*	*Placed*	*Unplaced*	*Total*	*Win %*	*Place %*
Hurdles	About 2m	1	2	9	12	8%	25%
	About 2m 4f	0	1	2	3	0%	33%
	About 3m	1	0	1	2	50%	50%
Chases	About 2m	0	0	0	0	-	-
	About 2m 4f	0	0	1	1	0%	0%
	About 3m	0	0	0	0	-	-
	About 4m	1	0	0	1	100%	100%
Bumper	About 2m	0	0	1	1	0%	0%
Total	**2008-2017**	**3**	**3**	**14**	**20**	**15%**	**30%**

Last year was a very satisfactory Cheltenham Festival for supporters of **Authorized**'s progeny. Two of the six **Authorized** bred entries came home winners and at the rewarding prices of 16/1 and 10/1.

The first of the offspring's runners to appear on the course was the *Gordon Elliott* trained ***Tiger Roll*** who was making his third visit to the Cheltenham Festival. Three years previously in 2014, as a four year old, ***Tiger Roll*** had been successful at odds of 10/1 in winning the *JCB Triumph Hurdle*. The victory kicked off a very special day for the horse's owners, *Gigginstown House Stud*, who later in the day secured three more winners to rack up an incredible 82,653/1 four timer. The following year, *Gordon Elliott* entered ***Tiger Roll*** in the *Ladbrokes World Hurdle* in which he finished 13th at a price of 50/1. It was the first hurdles race in which the five year old had raced over a distance of three miles. All his previous runs had been at around two miles.

Having missed the 2016 meeting, at last year's festival, ***Tiger Roll*** was entered in the opening day's penultimate race, the *JT McNamara National Hunt Challenge Cup Amateur Riders' Novices' Chase* over a distance of four miles. Just as in 2015, ***Tiger Roll*** was being tasked to compete in an event that was a mile further than any of the previous races in which he had contested. This time, however, the performance and result were very different as the 16/1 chance, under a positive ride by *Lisa O'Neill*, went clear at the last and stayed on up the hill to win by three lengths. It was the amateur jockey's first festival victory.

Also appearing for the third time at a festival last season was the *Willie Mullins* trained, ***Nichols Canyon***. On the previous two occasions, he had rewarded each way backers by finishing third in his races. Favourite for the *Neptune Investment Management Novices' Hurdle* in 2015, just as jockey *Ruby Walsh* started to galvanise ***Nichols Canyon***, the potential strong challenge petered out following a mistake at the second last hurdle. In 2016, ***Nichols Canyon*** was one of three *Willie Mullins* representatives for the 2016 *Stan James Champion Hurdle Challenge Trophy*, and the 15/2 chance had to settle for 3rd place for the second time at a festival, being no match for the stable's first string and favourite for the race, *Annie Power*, who made all and won easily. The third Cheltenham Festival contest for ***Nichols Canyon*** turned out to be his best performance as he came from off the pace to win the 2017 *Sun Bets Stayers' Hurdle* at 10/1. Tragically, later in the year, on 28th December, ***Nichols Canyon*** suffered a fatal fall in what was his 20th race over hurdles whilst racing in the *Squared Financial Christmas Hurdle* at *Leopardstown*. It was the third time in seven runs at *Leopardstown* where he had parted company with his jockey. In his other seventeen races, ***Nichols Canyon*** had never finished outside the front three.

In total, 14 of **Authorized**'s progeny have registered 20 festival appearances, and ***Tiger Roll*** and ***Nichols Canyon*** are two of three of the offspring to have appeared at the festival on three occasions, the other being ***Zamdy Man***. The gelding, trained by *Venetia Williams*, was purchased by *John P McManus* in December 2016 and had his first festival appearance in the owner's distinctive green-and-gold hooped racing colours at last year's festival. The change of ownership had little impact on the 12/1 chance who finished 10th and was never in contention in the *Close Brothers Novices' Handicap Chase*. ***Zamdy Man*** finished even further down the field in his two previous festival appearances; 12th in the 2013 *Fred Winter Juvenile Handicap Hurdle* and 18th in the 2016 *Vincent O'Brien County Handicap Hurdle*. The remaining eleven of **Authorized**'s stock have all participated at just one Cheltenham Festival and only one of them, ***Sternrubin***, has paid out on an each-way bet, when finishing 3rd at 33/1 in the 2016 *Vincent O'Brien County Handicap Hurdle*.

Up until now, had one had blindly backed all 20 festival runs from the offspring at £1.00 each way, the resultant profit would be £22.65, but the bulk of these profits are down to just two horses. To put this in perspective, had one backed just ***Tiger Roll*** and ***Nichols Canyon*** at previous festivals, the profit to a £1.00 each-way stake would be £41.40. Backing every other **Authorized** sired festival runner, without ***Tiger Roll*** and ***Nichols Canyon*** to the same stake would result in a loss of £18.75.

With only 20 festival runs on board, it would be rash to believe that current trends will continue to play out in the future, but it is interesting to note the current pattern which shows 90% of **Authorized** sired runners finishing either towards the back of the field or in the first three. Only two runners have registered a finishing position between 4th and 9th. A pessimistic explanation for this pattern could be that **Authorized**'s offspring typically have a very poor festival record, but two horses have turned out to be exceptional, ***Tiger Roll*** and ***Nichols Canyon*** being responsible for 5 of the 6 win and place positions. Without doubt, this is a very logical explanation but we will only know if the conclusion is accurate if festival wins and places dry up for this stallion in the future and all we see is a whole bunch of finishing positions of 10th or worse.

Bearing the above in mind, my head tells me that a watching brief on **Authorized**'s festival representatives is the best recommendation for the 2018 Cheltenham Festival. Even so, should there be an **Authorized** festival entry that I really like, my heart will probably rule my head and I will place my bet! In short, it's a difficult one, but with more data provided from future meetings, it will hopefully be easier to be more confident on whether or not **Authorized** is a stallion to follow.

Ballingarry (IRE)

Quote from the 2017 Cheltenham Festival Stallion Guide - "With just twelve festival runs to go on, there is nowhere near enough data on which to make foolhardy conclusions, but the performances at the 2016 Cheltenham Festival certainly provides **Ballingarry** supporters with some encouragement for the future."

Ballingarry (19-y-o)							
Race Format	*Miles*	*Won*	*Placed*	*Unplaced*	*Total*	*Win %*	*Place %*
Hurdles	About 2m	1	1	1	3	33%	67%
	About 2m 4f	0	0	5	5	0%	0%
	About 3m	0	0	2	2	0%	0%
Chases	About 2m	0	0	0	0	-	-
	About 2m 4f	0	1	1	2	0%	50%
	About 3m	0	0	2	2	0%	0%
	About 4m	0	0	0	0	-	-
Bumper	About 2m	0	0	0	0	-	-
Total	**2008-2017**	**1**	**2**	**11**	**14**	**7%**	**21%**

On the back of a victory, a place dividend and a 33/1 fifth placing from four **Ballingarry** sired runners at the 2016 Cheltenham Festival, I decided that the signs were encouraging enough to include **Ballingarry** in last year's Cheltenham Festival Stallion Guide, despite rather limited data upon which to determine any significant recommendations. So, I was rather disappointed that at last year's festival, only two of **Ballingarry**'s progeny turned up, both of whom provided rather nondescript performances.

The one festival winner of **Ballingarry**'s stock is ***Diego Du Charmil***, who at 13/2, just held on by a head from *Romain De Senam* in the 2016 *Fred Winter Juvenile Handicap Hurdle*. It was the second time that trainer *Paul Nicholls* was represented by a ***Ballingarry*** sired runner in this event for four year olds, as two years previously, he had entered the *Graham Wylie* owned, ***Katgary***, who put in a gallant effort to finish runner up behind 33/1 outsider *Hawk High*.

Diego Du Charmil attempted to follow up his 2016 victory in last season's *Randox Health County Handicap Hurdle*, but although the 12/1 chance was up with the chasing pack for most of the race, he faded as they approached the final flight and weakened to finish 12th. The other runner representing **Ballingarry** at the 2017 Cheltenham Festival was the *Nick Williams* trained ***Aubusson***. He was a huge price at 66/1 for the *Pertemps Network Final Handicap Hurdle* and ran accordingly, finishing in 16th position. Two years previously, he had finished just one from last at 50/1 in the *Ladbrokes World Hurdle*.

The only other festival performance from **Ballingarry**'s offspring that is worth a mention is ***Full Shift***'s 4th place dividend that was secured in the 2016 *Brown Advisory & Merriebelle Stable Plate*. The result was a definitive improvement on ***Full Shift***'s previous visits to the festival where he had twice competed in the *Martin Pipe Conditional Jockeys Handicap Hurdle*, finishing 11th in 2014 and 8th a year later.

It is perhaps worth noting that the win and both places from the 14 festival runs of **Ballingarry**'s progeny were achieved by runners who lined up at single figure odds, although the offspring certainly don't have a 100% record of market leaders always hitting a win or place. ***Balgarry*** was a 6/1 joint favourite when beaten into 7th in the 2012 *Coral Cup* and ***Full Shift*** was the 9/2 Favourite when disappointing with an 11th placing in the 2014 *Martin Pipe Conditional Jockeys' Handicap Hurdle*.

There have been seven festival runs from what can be considered as big price outsiders. By far the best performance of the seven, was ***Amigo*** (33/1) finishing in fifth place in the 2016 *Fulke Walwyn Kim Muir Challenge Cup Handicap Chase*. The other six **Ballingarry** representatives who raced at odds of 20/1 or bigger either failed to complete their races or finished 15th or worse.

With a disappointing turn-out of only two **Ballingarry** bred runners at last year's meeting and a total of just fourteen appearances on which to build any sort of analysis, I recommend a watching brief on the offspring until some meaningful trends emerge. For any reckless risk-takers out there, if you really want to bet on a **Ballingarry** runner at the 2018 Cheltenham Festival, then potentially the best place to look will be the *Boodles Fred Winter Juvenile Handicap Hurdle*, where in two attempts in this event to date, **Ballingarry** sired runners have registered a first and second. Finally, should it just so happen that a **Ballingarry** bred four year old does make the *Fred Winter* starting line-up, if the trainer of such horse turns out to be *Mr Paul Nicholls*, then perhaps I may even risk a wager myself!

Beneficial (GB)

Quote from the 2017 Cheltenham Festival Stallion Guide - "When it comes to the Cheltenham Festival, my strong recommendation to punters is to ignore **Beneficial**'s offspring completely unless there is a deluge of rain."

Beneficial (Died as a 23-y-o in 2013)								
Race Format	*Miles*	***Won***	***Placed***	***Unplaced***	***Total***	***Win %***	***Place %***
Hurdles	About 2m	0	0	7	7	0%	0%
	About 2m 4f	1	3	15	19	5%	21%
	About 3m	1	0	6	7	14%	14%
Chases	About 2m	0	4	13	17	0%	24%
	About 2m 4f	1	0	10	11	9%	9%
	About 3m	3	3	21	27	11%	22%
	About 4m	0	1	7	8	0%	13%
Bumper	About 2m	0	1	3	4	0%	25%
Total	**2008-2017**	**6**	**12**	**82**	**100**	**6%**	**18%**

As I was sipping a pint of Guinness before last year's *JT McNamara National Hunt Challenge Cup Amateur Riders' Novices' Chase*, my friend said to me, "They seem to fancy ***A Genie In Abottle***. It's 4/1 favourite. Just come in from 9/2." I looked up above me, held my hand out flat and replied, "It doesn't appear to be raining and I don't recall driving through torrential rain this morning either." My friend smiled. "I get it. He's out of **Beneficial**!"

I guess that punters were keen on the chances of ***A Genie In Abottle*** as he was to be partnered by *Jamie Codd*, the superb Irish amateur jockey, but even with *Mr Codd*'s undoubted assistance, the *Noel Meade* trained favourite made little impression on ground too lively for him and finished in fifth position, some 17 lengths behind the front four. Had it been raining heavily all day, I may well have been interested in backing ***A Genie In Abottle***, as **Beneficial**'s progeny have an excellent Cheltenham Festival record when there has been a deluge of rain. Conversely, without rain, the offspring can be safely ignored.

The past decade of results clearly support my assertion that **Beneficial**'s stock perform far better on soft to heavy going, so it was something of a surprise to see ***Monksland*** land a 4th place dividend in last year's *Coral Cup Handicap Hurdle*. *Noel Meade*'s triple Grade 2 hurdles winner was having his very first run in a handicap and stayed on well to claim 4th place at the rewarding odds of 66/1. It was ***Monksland***'s third run at a Cheltenham Festival. Two years earlier, he finished at the back of the field in the *Ladbrokes World Hurdle*, but on his first festival appearance, in 2012, he also recorded a place in the *Neptune Investment Management Novices' Hurdle*, when finishing a well beaten 3rd at odds of 11/2. ***Monksland***'s two hurdle placings is quite an achievement as, with the exception of Friday 15th March 2013 when it had been pouring with rain, he is the only one of **Beneficial**'s offspring to reward punters with a place dividend in any of the festival's 2½m hurdle contests.

I mention Friday 15th March 2013, as there was an avalanche of rain at the Cheltenham Festival on that day, with the rain lashing down from noon which resulted in the official going being changed to soft from the third race onwards. The only reward for **Beneficial** supporters in 2½m festival hurdle races, outside of ***Monksland***'s achievements highlighted above, occurred in the second last race of that Friday, the *Martin Pipe Conditional Jockeys' Handicap Hurdle*. The Paul Nicholls trained ***Salubrious*** won the race at 16/1 with the second **Beneficial** bred runner in the race, ***Make Your Mark*** securing the 4th place dividend at 8/1. It was a quick fire double for **Beneficial**'s offspring as in the previous race, as a result of *Oscar Delta* unshipping jockey, *Jane Mangan*, 150 yards from the finish, ***Salsify*** became the fortuitous winner of the *CGA Foxhunter Chase Challenge Cup*. In the festival's last race, the *Nicky Henderson* trained ***Kid Cassidy*** did his best to give **Beneficial** supporters a hat trick of wins, but he was unable to quicken when it mattered and finished runner-up, at odds of 12/1, in the *Johnny Henderson Grand Annual Chase Challenge Cup*.

Roll forward two years and Gold Cup day suffered heavy rain for the second time in three years, and once again, **Beneficial**'s offspring prospered, with the soft going helping two of the four **Beneficial** bred runners to record runner-up spots. There were two entries in the *St. James's Place Foxhunter Chase Challenge Cup*, one of whom was ***Salsify*** (10/1) who had already won the *Foxhunters* twice in 2012 and 2013. He was eventually pulled up in the race four from home, but the other **Beneficial** sired runner, ***Following Dreams***, managed to finish second at the rewarding odds of 50/1, some 17 lengths behind the *Nina Carberry* ridden, *On The Fringe*. The other two of **Beneficial**'s offspring to take part on the Friday were entered in the festival's final race - the *A.P. McCoy Grand Annual Chase Challenge Cup*, and it was the *Jonjo O'Neill* trained 12/1 shot, ***Eastlake***, who finished runner-up four lengths behind *Next Sensation*. The other **Beneficial** bred runner, ***Mount Colah*** (25/1), was pulled up two from home when tailed off.

Backing all eleven **Beneficial** sired runners, who ran on soft ground following the torrential downpours of 15th March 2013 and 13th March 2015, would have provided an excellent profit of £26.40 to a £1.00 each-way stake. Compare this profit, and the two wins and four places achieved, with the remaining 89 of **Beneficial** bred contenders since the 2008 festival onwards, who took part in races without the benefit of heavy rain. Of the 89 festival runners, just four won and eight were placed and staking a £1.00 each-way bet on all of them blind would have delivered a rather painful £91.10 loss.

Before ***Monksland***'s 4th place finish in last year's *Coral Cup Handicap Hurdle*, the only **Beneficial** bred horse to enter Cheltenham's Winners Enclosure in the last four festival meetings (excluding the wet day of 13th March 2015) is ***More Of That***. In 2016, ***More Of That*** lined up in the *RSA Chase* as the 6/4 favourite, but having suffered broken blood vessels in the latter stages of the race, could only finish 3rd. It was better news for the *Jonjo O'Neill* trained gelding at the 2014 Cheltenham Festival, when at odds of 15/2, *Barry Geraghty* rode ***More Of That*** to a 1½ length victory ahead of *Annie Power* in the *Ladbrokes World Hurdle*. In summary, if we ignore 13th March 2015, **Beneficial**'s progeny have been represented on 47 occasions in the past four Cheltenham Festivals and have recorded just one victory and two places, all three courtesy of the aforementioned ***Monksland*** and ***More Of That***. Of the remaining 44 appearances from the offspring, 36 runners ended up a long way behind the leaders, registering finishing positions of 8th or worse.

Over the past few years, the festival performances of **Beneficial**'s progeny have achieved nothing other than to strengthen my views about the stallion. In short, if there is torrential rain at the festival that causes the going to be changed to soft or worse, punters should be very interested in the offspring's runners and each way bets on them may well produce profitable rewards. On the other hand, if you can't see umbrellas, raincoats or wellie boots as you excitedly make your way towards Cheltenham, then all **Beneficial** bred entries can be disregarded.

Califet (FR)

Califet was not featured in the 2017 Cheltenham Festival Stallion Guide.

Califet (20-y-o)							
Race Format	*Miles*	***Won***	***Placed***	***Unplaced***	***Total***	***Win %***	***Place %***
Hurdles	About 2m	0	0	4	4	0%	0%
	About 2m 4f	0	0	2	2	0%	0%
	About 3m	0	0	1	1	0%	0%
Chases	About 2m	0	0	2	2	0%	0%
	About 2m 4f	0	0	1	1	-	-
	About 3m	0	0	1	1	0%	0%
	About 4m	0	0	0	0	-	-
Bumper	About 2m	0	0	0	0	-	-
Total	**2008-2017**	**0**	**0**	**11**	**11**	**0%**	**0%**

Seven of **Califet**'s offspring have registered just 11 festival appearances. None have won. None have placed. All of which begs the question as to why this stallion has made it into the 2018 Cheltenham Festival Guide? Obviously, it is difficult to determine any definitive conclusions based upon so few runs, but my early analysis suggests that it won't be too long before **Califet**'s offspring are successful in securing a top three finish.

Within the progeny's 11 runs, **Califet** sired festival runners have competed in 7 hurdle events and 4 chases. When it comes to the distance travelled in these 11 appearances, the results are so far suggesting that **Califet**'s offspring perform best over the minimum distance of two miles. The best set of results are in the 2m hurdle category where in four runs to date, **Califet**'s representatives have been knocking on the door of claiming a place position. The first of the stock to appear in a festival two mile hurdle contest was ***Clarcam*** in 2014. There are numerous examples in racing where one is jumping up and down with excitement one moment and then down in the mouth a few seconds later. I imagine all racing fans have experienced these feelings. Punters who had placed an each way bet on ***Clarcam***, at 16/1, were probably starting to get excited as their selection, still travelling strongly, moved into the lead in the 2014 *Fred Winter Juvenile Handicap Hurdle*. Their hopes were dashed two from home as ***Clarcam*** suffered a crashing fall which was particularly awful for jockey *Bryan Cooper* who unfortunately was out of the saddle for the next few months having sustained a broken leg with a fractured right tibia and fibula.

Later at that meeting, in Friday's opening race, **Califet** was represented by 11/2 favourite, ***Calipto***, in the only other festival event restricted to four year olds, the *JCB Triumph Hurdle*. Bizarrely, further misfortune was to strike **Califet**'s progeny once again, this time due to ***Calipto***'s stirrup leather breaking approaching two out. Without irons, it was hugely difficult for jockey *Daryl Jacob* to provide any major help to ***Calipto*** who carried on running throughout the rest of the race to finish in 4th place. Before the stirrup leather broke, the *Paul Nicholls* trained favourite was travelling smoothly, so one does wonder what may have happened had *Daryl Jacob* been able to compete on equal terms with the first three home.

Looking at the re-run of the 2015 *Vincent O'Brien County Handicap Hurdle*, one can be forgiven for thinking that there may be a jinx against **Califet**'s festival two mile hurdle runners. The *Willie Mullins* trained ***Analifet*** was making good headway towards the business end of the race, only to hang to her left on the run-in and lose two places in the final 120 yards. If the 33/1 mare had stayed on straight, she almost certainly would have claimed 3rd position and a place dividend.

The 4th two mile hurdle festival contest in which a **Califet** sired runner competed was in last year's opening event, the *Sky Bet Supreme Novices' Hurdle*. Trainer *Willie Mullins* had decided to try a first-time hood for his entry, ***Cilaos Emery***, but it didn't appear to help too much as the 12/1 chance was once again very keen and soon in the lead, finding it difficult to settle. He was eventually headed two from home and weakened to finish in 5th place. No bad luck this time, although he reportedly did lose a right hand shoe.

Having had a runner in the opening event at last year's Cheltenham Festival, perhaps it was fitting that a **Califet** representative would also hold an entry in the meeting's closing event, the *Johnny Henderson Grand Annual Challenge Cup Handicap Chase*. The aforementioned ***Calipto***, who had finished 4th in the 2014 *Triumph Hurdle*, had changed owner and trainer just one month before the 2017 *Grand Annual*, moving from *Paul Nicholls' Ditcheat* yard to *Venetia Williams*' stables in Herefordshire. On his debut for his new connections, ***Calipto*** put in a very good effort to finish in 6th place at a price of 14/1.

The one other appearance from **Califet**'s offspring at last year's festival was a third festival appearance from ***Clarcam***, who had put in a dismal effort in the 2015 *Racing Post Arkle Challenge Trophy*, a year after his fall in the 2014 *Fred Winter*. Having missed the 2016 Cheltenham Festival, ***Clarcam*** returned last year in the 3m1f *Ultima Handicap Chase*. He was unfancied at 50/1 and finished in 9th place. He wasn't helped by being severely hampered at the very first flight due to the fall of *Caid Du Berlais*. It is worth noting that of the five runs from **Califet**'s stock in festival races that are 2½ miles or more, ***Clarcam***'s 9th position is actually the highest recorded, the other four attempts resulting in 11th, 13th, 16th and ***Bivouac*** being pulled up in the 2016 *Martin Pipe Conditional Jockeys' Handicap Hurdle*.

Albeit that the data is limited based on so few runs, as we approach the 2018 Cheltenham Festival, unless one considers **Califet**'s stock to be jinxed, the early signs suggest that the offspring are worth supporting in the festival's two mile hurdle events. As for every other race category, my advice is that we watch and learn.

Cape Cross (IRE)

Quote from the 2017 Cheltenham Festival Stallion Guide - "I would not necessarily dissuade anyone from supporting the progeny, as one cannot be too negative about the achievement of 3 places from 18 runs, especially in light of the starting prices of 12/1, 25/1 and 50/1. That said, as far as **Cape Cross**'s stock goes, I will probably keep my money in my pocket."

Cape Cross (Died as a 23-y-o in 2017)							
Race Format	*Miles*	***Won***	***Placed***	***Unplaced***	***Total***	***Win %***	***Place %***
Hurdles	About 2m	0	1	12	13	0%	8%
	About 2m 4f	0	1	4	5	0%	20%
	About 3m	0	0	1	1	0%	0%
Chases	About 2m	0	0	0	0	-	-
	About 2m 4f	0	0	1	1	0%	0%
	About 3m	0	0	0	0	-	-
	About 4m	0	0	0	0	-	-
Bumper	About 2m	0	0	0	0	-	-
Total	**2008-2017**	**0**	**2**	**18**	**20**	**0%**	**10%**

Sadly, in April 2017, **Cape Cross** died at the age of 23 following complications associated with old age. **Cape Cross** was essentially a sire of flat racehorses and is one of only 17 stallions to have sired more than one *Derby* winner. He was a central part of *Godolphin* and *Darley*'s global breeding operations and stood at *Kildangan Stud* in Ireland.

As for his offspring that went jumping over fences and hurdles, fifteen of them have raced at the Cheltenham Festival competing in a total of 22 races, only two of which took place more than ten years ago. **Cape Cross** has still not produced a Cheltenham Festival winner, but three of the progeny have managed to secure a place dividend. The first of these was in 2006 when ***Artist's Muse***, trained by *Ted Walsh* and ridden by his son, *Ruby*, finished 2nd at odds of 12/1 in the 2006 *Fred Winter Juvenile Novices' Handicap Hurdle*. There was a seven year wait before the next festival placing by a **Cape Cross** bred runner, and it occurred in the 2013 *Vincent O'Brien County Handicap Hurdle*, when ***Manyriverstocross*** registered a third placing at odds of 25/1. The biggest priced placed horse at a Cheltenham Festival for **Cape Cross** followers occurred in the 2016 *Martin Pipe Conditional Jockeys' Handicap Hurdle*, where ***Sky Khan***, trained by *Lucinda Russell*, claimed 3rd place at the rewarding odds of 50/1.

Of the 22 **Cape Cross** bred runners who lined up in their festival races, nine of them were sent off at odds of 33/1 or bigger with the highest placing achieved from these nine outsiders, bar ***Sky Khan***'s 3rd placing, being eleventh. Only in two festival races has a **Cape Cross** representative returned a price of less than 10/1, one of which was on the sole occasion that a **Cape Cross** bred runner competed in a festival chase, all of the other 21 appearances taking place over hurdles. In his 4th race over fences, in the 2014 *Rewards4Racing Novices' Handicap Chase*, ***Manyriverstocross*** who had finished 3rd in the previous year's *County Hurdle*, weakened towards the end of the race and came home in 7th position, ten lengths off the winner at a price of 17/2.

The shortest priced **Cape Cross** sired festival runner competed in last year's *Fred Winter Juvenile Handicap Hurdle*. There was a big gamble on the *John Joseph Hanlon* trained, ***Linger***, who opened in the betting at 14/1, but as the bets rained in, his price had halved to 7/1 at the off. As is often the case, the gamble didn't pay off. ***Linger*** disappointed and was pulled up lame before three out. Ten of the offspring have raced at the festival as four year olds and ***Linger***'s performance has been the worst of all of them. If we discount the two huge priced outsiders of ***Kuilsriver*** (125/1) and ***Cape Explorer*** (100/1) both of whom ran in *Triumph*, then we are left with eight **Cape Cross** juveniles, four which raced in the *Fred Winter* and four in the *Triumph*. Starting with the *Fred Winter*, the previously mentioned runner-up spot by ***Artist's Muse*** at 12/1 is the best result and ***Linger***'s pulled up effort at 7/1 is the worst. In between, two 14/1 chances finished 12th and 7th. As for the *Triumph Hurdle*, the **Cape Cross** participants have been knocking at the door, finishing just outside the places on all four occasions. In 2005, ***Diego Cao*** finished 7th at 20/1; In 2010, ***Gilded Age*** was placed 6th at 28/1; In 2015, ***Devilment*** (16/1) was 4th behind a *Nicky Henderson* trained 1-2-3; and in 2016, ***Leoncavello*** finished 5th at 18/1. Nine of the progeny have competed in the festival's handicap hurdles for older horses, two of whom registered a third place as already highlighted. As for the other seven runners, all of them finished 10th or worse.

In thinking about the forthcoming festival, it is still early days on which to base any firm conclusions, especially given that the majority of **Cape Cross**'s 22 festival runners have been outsiders. There is a possibility that a big priced selection may pop up to reward supporters, as already demonstrated by three of the 22 **Cape Cross** representatives to date registering a place. And perhaps 2018 will be the year when one of the progeny's four year old runners manages to hit a top three position in the *Triumph Hurdle*. Nevertheless, on balance, I think this is more hope than expectation. The numbers don't lie and had one backed all 22 of the offspring's festival runners so far to a £1.00 each way stake, the outcome would be a loss of £19.25. Until there is evidence to the contrary, for the 2018 Cheltenham Festival, my recommendation is to strike a line through all **Cape Cross** sired entries.

Definite Article (GB)

Quote from the 2017 Cheltenham Festival Stallion Guide - "I guess there is a possibility that the progeny's performances may improve to pre-2007 levels, but for now, there is only one conclusion to be made. Strike out all **Definite Article** bred entries who line up at the 2017 Cheltenham Festival."

Definite Article (26-y-o)							
Race Format	*Miles*	***Won***	***Placed***	***Unplaced***	***Total***	***Win %***	***Place %***
Hurdles	About 2m	0	0	2	2	0%	0%
	About 2m 4f	0	0	3	3	0%	0%
	About 3m	0	0	5	5	0%	0%
Chases	About 2m	0	0	2	2	0%	0%
	About 2m 4f	0	0	1	1	0%	0%
	About 3m	0	0	3	3	0%	0%
	About 4m	0	0	1	1	0%	0%
Bumper	About 2m	0	0	4	4	0%	0%
Total	**2008-2017**	**0**	**0**	**21**	**21**	**0%**	**0%**

The only time that I have left the Cheltenham Festival by public transport was in 2006 when I took a National Express coach into London. Back then, the last race on the Friday was the *Vincent O'Brien County Handicap Hurdle*, a race I couldn't stay for, otherwise I would have missed the coach. As the runners lined up for the penultimate race of the meeting, following a number of losing bets and having just a few pounds in my pocket, I remember thinking that I would need to go to a cashpoint - unless I was lucky enough to collect some winnings from my last bet of the day, which rested on the shoulders of a *Nicky Henderson* trained 20/1 chance in the *Johnny Henderson Grand Annual Chase Challenge Cup*. Luckily for me, ***Greenhope***, sired by **Definite Article**, won by two lengths and saved the day. Having collected my winnings, I rushed off to catch my bus.

I've no idea why I had backed ***Greenhope***. It certainly had nothing to do with the fact that he was out of **Definite Article**. I didn't take too much attention to a runner's sire in those days. But the 2006 meeting turned out to be very successful for anyone who had decided to support the three festival runners sired by **Definite Article**, as two of them won. Both winners were trained by *Nicky Henderson*. The day before ***Greenhope***'s victory, in the *Racing Post Plate*, a Grade 3 handicap chase over 2m5f, ***Non So*** cruised to a 9 length victory at a price of 14/1. Three years earlier, in 2003, ***Non So*** picked up a festival place position when finishing 4th in the *Vincent O'Brien County Hurdle*.

As it is now 2018, some of you may be questioning why on earth are you reading about **Definite Article**'s offspring going back twelve years and more? The answer is simple. Since 2006, with regard to the festival performances of **Definite Article**'s progeny, there isn't anything of note to write about. All 23 festival runners sired by **Definite Article** since 2006 have failed to register a win or place. Indeed, overall, the performances have been abysmal. At last year's festival, it was more of the same. In the opening event of the festival, the *Sky Bet Supreme Novices' Hurdle*, ***Pingshou*** (25/1) finished 10th of 14 runners. In the very last race of the meeting, ***Sizing Platinum*** (20/1) was 19th out of the 24 who set off in the *Johnny Henderson Grand Annual Challenge Cup Handicap Chase*. In between these two races, ***Perfect Harmony*** (33/1) never troubled the leaders either when finishing 11th in the *Weatherbys Champion Bumper*.

In total, there have been 32 festival appearances from **Definite Article**'s offspring, of which 21 have taken place within the past ten years. The record of **Definite Article** sired runners within the first five festivals in which they competed was very good. Out of a total of nine runs between 2002 and 2006, the progeny recorded two wins, one place, a 5th, 6th and 8th. However, since then, results have been truly awful. In the eleven Cheltenham Festivals from 2007 onwards, only three of the 23 **Definite Article** bred runners have registered a top ten finish; ***Definity*** (3/1 favourite) finished 5th in the 2011 *Centenary Novices' Handicap Chase*; ***Virginia Ash*** was 7th in the 2013 *Albert Bartlett Novices' Hurdle*; and ***Definitly Red*** finished 7th in the 2014 *Weatherbys Champion Bumper*.

In your 2018 Festival calculations, discount all entries sired by **Definite Article**.

Dom Alco (FR)

Quote from the 2017 Cheltenham Festival Stallion Guide - "**Dom Alco**'s progeny tend to perform reasonably well at Cheltenham Festivals. But not well enough to win. At the past 10 festivals, twenty of the 41 runs have resulted in a top six finish, including two wins, five seconds, one third and no fewer than six fourth place finishes."

Dom Alco (Died as a 23-y-o in 2010)							
Race Format	*Miles*	*Won*	*Placed*	*Unplaced*	*Total*	*Win %*	*Place %*
Hurdles	About 2m	1	0	2	3	33%	33%
	About 2m 4f	1	1	5	7	14%	29%
	About 3m	0	2	0	2	0%	100%
Chases	About 2m	0	0	2	2	0%	0%
	About 2m 4f	0	1	5	6	0%	17%
	About 3m	0	2	14	16	0%	13%
	About 4m	0	0	6	6	0%	0%
Bumper	About 2m	0	1	0	1	0%	100%
Total	**2008-2017**	**2**	**7**	**34**	**43**	**5%**	**21%**

In the past decade of Cheltenham Festivals, **Dom Alco** has been the sire of thirty runners in the festival's chase events. Ten of those thirty participants, or exactly one third of them, have secured a top four finish. Before rushing down to your local bookmaker to place substantial wagers on **Dom Alco**'s progeny at the 2018 Cheltenham Festival, you may wish to know that backing all 30 runners blind to a £1.00 each-way stake would have resulted in a substantial loss of £47.00.

The crux of the matter is that despite **Dom Alco**'s progeny performing reasonably well at Cheltenham Festivals, they don't appear capable of winning. If **Dom Alco** was a Premier League Football Team, he would be Everton or Southampton – usually up there in the top half of the table but not equipped to break into the top six. When it comes to festival chase events, **Dom Alco** is extremely good at finishing fourth. In 30 chase appearances over the past ten years, **Dom Alco**'s representatives have finished 4th on no less than seven occasions, close to a 25% hit-rate! And every single 4th place achieved over the bigger obstacles has occurred in a non-handicap contest, so no place dividend for those unfortunate enough to have placed an each-way bet. So, although it is one-third of **Dom Alco** bred runners to have secured a top four finish in the festival chase events over the past decade, none of them won and only three have finished 2nd or 3rd.

The most recent placing over fences for **Dom Alco**'s progeny occurred at last year's meeting, something that had not been achieved at a Cheltenham Festival since 2008, the year in which ***New Alco*** came to be the very first of the offspring to achieve a place when he took the runner-up spot in the *William Hill Trophy Handicap Chase*. Three days later and ***Neptune Collonges*** became the second of **Dom Alco**'s stock to reward supporters with a place dividend, when finishing third in the 2008 *Totesport Cheltenham Gold Cup Chase*. It was quite an occasion for *Paul Nicholls*, the trainer of ***Neptune Collonges***, as he secured a 1-2-3 in the blue riband contest, with the esteemed *Denman* getting the better of his equally famed stablemate *Kauto Star*.

It was ***Baron Alco***, trained by *Gary Moore*, who finally ended eight blank years in festival chase events for **Dom Alco**'s stock. *Jamie Moore*, ***Baron Alco***'s rider, had the 10/1 chance prominent throughout, setting a strong pace from the 8th and then staying on gamely up the Cheltenham Hill to finish second behind *Road To Respect*, who once he had overcome a scare early on when over-jumping the very first fence, won relatively comfortably by six lengths.

As well as ***Baron Alco***, there were three other **Dom Alco** sired festival entries last year. ***Vic De Touzaine*** (25/1) unseated two out when his stamina had emptied in the *Ultima Handicap Chase* and ***Unioniste***, trained by *Paul Nicholls*, finished 9th in Thursday's *Fulke Walwyn Kim Muir Challenge Cup Amateur Riders' Handicap Chase* at a price of 33/1. The other **Dom Alco** bred runner to take his chance last year was also trained by *Paul Nicholls*, the 12/1 chance ***Arpege D'Alene***, who finished (you've guessed it) in 4th position in the *JT McNamara National Hunt Challenge Cup Amateur Riders' Novices' Chase*. ***Arpege D'Alene***'s next appearance was in the *Coral Scottish Grand National Handicap Chase* at *Ayr*, where sadly for connections, he was pulled up quickly before the 11th fence and had to be put down.

When one looks at the results of **Dom Alco**'s stock at Cheltenham Festivals, it is rather bizarre that in 36 races over fences, the offspring have a dismal place strike rate of 8% having achieved just three place positions. And yet, when it comes to the smaller obstacles, despite having been entered in just 13 hurdle races, **Dom Alco**'s progeny have achieved a win strike rate of 15% and a win and place strike rate of 46%. The most profitable race category for **Dom Alco**'s offspring is undoubtedly in the festival's three mile hurdle events. The aforementioned ***Arpege D'Alene*** finished second to *Mall Dini* in the 2016 *Pertemps Network Final*; ***Grand Crus*** was also a runner-up in the 2011 *Ladbrokes World Hurdle*; and fourteen years ago in the 2003 renewal of the *Pertemps Final*, ***Tribal Venture***, at 33/1, became the very first of the progeny to line up in a Cheltenham Festival event and a successful debut for **Dom Alco**'s stock it was, as the *Ferdy Murphy* trained five year old finished third. All of which adds up to **Dom Alco** sired runners having a 100% place record in the festival's 3m hurdle events.

Despite the encouraging statistics in the festival's hurdle races, any future appearances from **Dom Alco**'s progeny in these contests are likely to be few and far between. It would appear that most trainers are keen to put their **Dom Alco** bred horses over fences sooner rather than later and with **Dom Alco**'s passing in 2010, the progeny's runners are now seven or older, hence the likelihood that from now on, the offspring will invariably be entered in the longer distance chase events.

Based upon the historic trend of **Dom Alco**'s stock failing to register a single chase victory and repeatedly just missing out on securing a place dividend, the recommendation is to give **Dom Alco** sired chase entries the cold shoulder. On the other hand, if you spot one of **Dom Alco**'s offspring amongst the list of runners in a festival hurdle event, then you should be very interested, especially if the contest is over a distance of three miles.

For a whimsical footnote, if you can find a friendly bookmaker who is happy to take on peculiar wagers, how about requesting a bet on **Dom Alco** bred runners finishing in fourth position in the festival's non-handicap chase events!

Dr Massini (IRE)

Quote from the 2017 Cheltenham Festival Stallion Guide - "Although there have been many inauspicious performances from the progeny of **Dr Massini**, every so often, we witness a very good performance and often at big prices."

Dr Massini (Died as a 24-y-o in 2017)							
Race Format	*Miles*	*Won*	*Placed*	*Unplaced*	*Total*	*Win %*	*Place %*
Hurdles	About 2m	0	1	1	2	0%	50%
	About 2m 4f	0	0	4	4	0%	0%
	About 3m	0	0	2	2	0%	0%
Chases	About 2m	0	0	2	2	0%	0%
	About 2m 4f	0	2	3	5	0%	40%
	About 3m	0	2	6	8	0%	25%
	About 4m	0	0	1	1	0%	0%
Bumper	About 2m	0	0	1	1	0%	0%
Total	**2008-2017**	**0**	**5**	**20**	**25**	**0%**	**20%**

The very first of **Dr Massini**'s progeny to race at the Cheltenham Festival was the *Philip Hobbs* trained, ***Massini's Maguire***, who sprang a surprise when *Richard Johnson* rode him to victory in the 2007 *Ballymore Properties Novices' Hurdle* at 20/1. Since then, over the next ten years, a further 17 of the offspring have made 25 festival appearances in an effort to add another victory to that early success. All have failed.

There is a rather strange pattern to the profile of this stallion's festival representatives. Typically, a **Dr Massini** bred festival runner will finish towards the tail end of the field in its festival race and a fair few won't complete the contest due to a fall or being pulled up. However, every now and then, the odd participant will surprise us and run into a place, and usually at a big price. Supporting **Dr Massini**'s festival representatives is therefore hugely frustrating, a little like being a fan of a struggling football team that you expect to lose every time you watch them, and then every so often, your team will pull off a shock away win at one of the top clubs. And to continue the analogy, your team pulls off just enough surprise away wins to successfully avoid relegation; just like you would make a profit if you had backed to level stakes all 26 festival appearances of **Dr Massini**'s offspring!

At last year's festival, there were three **Dr Massini** sired festival entries at odds of 100/1, 50/1 and 6/1 favourite. And if you take into account the stallion's festival record as advised above, the conclusion to be drawn is to ignore the starting prices, and assume that they all have an equal chance of success. As it turned out, no surprise away wins at the 2017 Cheltenham Festival! The 6/1 favourite was the *Nigel Twiston-Davies* trained, ***Foxtail Hill***, who fell at the 8th fence in the *Close Brothers Novices' Handicap Chase*; ***Massini's Trap*** at 100/1 finished 14th in the *Martin Pipe Conditional Jockeys' Handicap Hurdle*; and probably the best performance was ***Forgotten Gold***'s 10th place finish in the *Fulke Walwyn Kim Muir Challenge Cup Amateur Riders' Handicap Chase*, where at least the 50/1 outsider was in the leading bunch until weakening two fences from home.

The results from last year, therefore, were very much in sync with the previous 23 performances from the progeny. To date, if we take all 26 festival results from **Dr Massini**'s bred runners, we have seven runners that failed to complete their races; seven that finished in 10th place or worse; five that recorded finishing positions between 6th and 9th; two that finished 4th (one of which registered a place dividend); and five top 3 finishes, one of which was a victory. Perhaps, surprisingly, if you had placed a £1.00 each way bet on all 26 of these runs, you would now be £14.50 better off.

This £14.50 profit has been significantly influenced by just three results, these being the previously highlighted ***Massini's Maguire*** 20/1 success in the 2007 *Ballymore Properties Novices' Hurdle*; ***Glam Gerry***'s 3rd place finish in the 2012 *Byrne Group Plate* at a price of 33/1; and in the 2013 renewal of the *Jewson Novices' Chase*, the 3rd place finish of 100/1 outsider, ***Changing Times***. These three results provide 84% of all winnings returned had one wagered each-way level stakes bets on all of **Dr Massini** sired festival runners.

Even though betting on **Dr Massini**'s progeny at Cheltenham Festivals has so far been profitable, watching the offspring's performances from the stands can only be described as a somewhat disappointing and depressing experience, interspersed with moments of exhilarating joy. Unfortunately, with this stallion, those feelings of elation when you have picked a big priced winner or placed horse has only been experienced three times in eleven years. Despite the profits, that isn't often enough for me and so, at this year's festival, I will be giving **Dr Massini** sired entries the cold shoulder.

Flemensfirth (USA)

Quote from the 2017 Cheltenham Festival Stallion Guide - "Even though the performances from **Flemensfirth**'s offspring may have been encouraging preceding 2011, the current advice to punters could not be more emphatic. Steer clear of the progeny until we see a clear turnaround in recent trends."

Flemensfirth (26-y-o)								
Race Format	*Miles*	*Won*	*Placed*	*Unplaced*	*Total*	*Win %*	*Place %*
Hurdles	About 2m	0	0	3	3	0%	0%
	About 2m 4f	0	4	16	20	0%	20%
	About 3m	0	2	9	11	0%	18%
Chases	About 2m	1	0	2	3	33%	33%
	About 2m 4f	1	3	9	13	8%	31%
	About 3m	1	2	19	22	5%	14%
	About 4m	0	1	13	14	0%	7%
Bumper	About 2m	0	0	7	7	0%	0%
Total	**2008-2017**	**3**	**12**	**78**	**93**	**3%**	**16%**

Although it was certainly not a major turnaround in results, at least the 2017 Cheltenham Festival represented the best set of results for **Flemensfirth** sired runners since 2013. In total, for the three years preceding last season, **Flemensfirth**'s progeny had lined up in 35 races of which there were just two runner-up spots and a further 30 horses that were unable to finish higher than 8th. So, last season's festival record of two 3rd place dividends and a 5th placing from just nine **Flemensfirth** bred runners, although unprofitable, was certainly an improvement. For the record, if one had backed blind all nine of the progeny at the 2017 meeting, it would have resulted in a loss of £12.38 to a £1.00 each-way stake. The last time that **Flemensfirth**'s offspring provided punters with two or more winning festival each-way bets was in 2013, where if one had placed a £1.00 each-way bet on all eight of **Flemensfirth** bred runners that year, the three places achieved would have delivered a loss of £3.70.

The last festival meeting in which supporting all of **Flemensfirth**'s stock blind would have been profitable, was the year in which *Paddy Brennan* rode ***Imperial Commander*** to victory over the *Paul Nicholls* trained pair of *Kauto Star* and *Denman* in what was a memorable *Totesport Cheltenham Gold Cup Chase*. Based upon the festival record of the progeny preceding that memorable race in 2010, very few would have predicted eight years later, that we would still be awaiting the next **Flemensfirth** sired festival winner.

Imperial Commander is one of only two of **Flemensfirth**'s offspring to register two Cheltenham Festival victories. The year before his *Gold Cup* success, he was victorious in the 2009 *Ryanair Chase*, staying on gamely to beat the *Alan King* trained odds-on favourite, *Voy Por Ustedes*, by 2 lengths. Preceding the achievements of ***Imperial Commander***, the only other **Flemensfirth** sired horse to record two Cheltenham Festival wins is the *Venetia Williams* trained, ***Idole First***, who passed the winning post in first place at 33/1 in the 2005 *Coral Cup* and at 12/1 in the 2007 *Racing Post Plate*.

As well as ***Idole First*** and ***Imperial Commander***, four other **Flemensfirth** sired runners have managed to finish in the front three twice at Cheltenham Festivals, three of them before 2010. The *Paul Nicholls* trained, ***Kicks For Free***, finished 3rd in the 2006 *Weatherbys Champion Bumper* before taking the runner-up position in the 2008 *Coral Cup*, agonisingly just a nose away from the winner, *Naiad Du Misselot*. In the same year, ***Tidal Bay*** was victorious in the *Irish Independent Arkle Challenge Trophy Chase*, a year after finishing runner-up to *Massini's Maguire* in the 2007 *Ballymore Properties Novices' Hurdle*. And ***The Midnight Club*** took 3rd position in consecutive years in the 2009 *Albert Bartlett Novices' Hurdle* and the 2010 *Jewson Novices' Handicap Chase*.

It took seven years before we would witness the sixth of **Flemensfirth**'s offspring to record two festival top three finishes, when at last year's meeting, the *Gordon Elliott* trained, ***Noble Endeavor*** registered a 3rd placing in the *Ultima Handicap Chase* at odds of 15/2. Two years previously, with apprentice jockey, *Kevin Sexton*, in the saddle, ***Noble Endeavor*** was beaten in the final stride by *Killultagh Vic* who rallied well to win by a head, the 2015 *Martin Pipe Conditional Jockeys' Handicap Hurdle*.

Four festival races after the 2017 *Ultima Handicap Chase* in which ***Noble Endeavour*** registered a place dividend, we witnessed another 3rd place finish for **Flemensfirth**'s offspring in the final race of the day, when ***Two Taffs*** at odds of 7/1, finished behind winner *Tully East* and runner-up *Gold Present*, in the *Close Brothers Novices' Handicap Chase*. It was ***Two Taffs*** fourth race over fences and in an effort to gain a first chase victory, trainer *Dan Skelton* decided to run the 7 year old gelding with first time cheekpieces and tongue-tie. Despite being badly hampered mid-way through the race, ***Two Taffs*** was given a patient ride by *Davy Russell*, gradually creeping into the race and keeping on, but without the pace to catch the front two. The following month, ***Two Taffs*** lost his maiden tag when winning the Listed *Hillhouse Quarry Handicap Chase* at *Ayr*.

It was on St. Patrick's Day 2004, in the *Weatherbys Champion Bumper*, in which the first two of **Flemensfirth**'s offspring were to appear at a Cheltenham Festival. ***Major Vernon*** finished 13th in the race but the *Thomas Cooper* bay mare, ***Total Enjoyment***, travelled smoothly throughout the race and won comfortably at odds of 7/1. If one had placed a £1.00 each-way bet on these two *Bumper* runners and every single **Flemensfirth** bred festival representative up to and including ***Imperial Commander***'s victory in the 2010 *Totesport Cheltenham Gold Cup Chase*, then the 7 winners and 8 places from 38 festival appearances would have delivered a profit of £71.20. Since then, however, from 70 further festival outings, **Flemensfirth**'s offspring have managed just eight place positions and have failed to register a victory. Backing all 70 blind would have resulted in a £100.58 loss to a £1.00 each-way stake, wiping out the previous seven years' worth of profit.

I love to reminisce about Cheltenham Festivals in years gone by and I have many fond memories of **Flemensfirth** sired runners preceding 2011. But supporting horses simply for nostalgic reasons is unlikely to provide financial rewards, and in **Flemensfirth**'s case, supporting the stock over the past seven years has been highly unprofitable. At the 2018 Cheltenham Festival, boycotting the progeny can be the only sensible prescription.

Galileo (IRE)

Quote from the 2017 Cheltenham Festival Stallion Guide - "With **Galileo** being a young stallion of 19 years old, there is a good chance that at forthcoming Cheltenham Festivals, every so often, one of his offspring will pop up out of the blue and record a festival win or place. However, for every winner, there will be a whole bunch of losers, many of which will finish well down the field."

Galileo (20-y-o)							
Race Format	*Miles*	*Won*	*Placed*	*Unplaced*	*Total*	*Win %*	*Place %*
Hurdles	About 2m	1	1	16	18	6%	11%
	About 2m 4f	2	0	7	9	22%	22%
	About 3m	0	1	4	5	0%	20%
Chases	About 2m	0	0	0	0	-	-
	About 2m 4f	0	0	0	0	-	-
	About 3m	0	0	0	0	-	-
	About 4m	0	0	0	0	-	-
Bumper	About 2m	0	0	2	2	0%	0%
Total	**2008-2017**	**3**	**2**	**29**	**34**	**9%**	**15%**

If we look at the results of **Galileo**'s stock overall, 24 of the progeny have registered 35 Cheltenham Festival runs between them with all bar one of the appearances taking place within the past decade. Aside from two sixth place efforts in the *Weatherbys Champion Bumper*, all of **Galileo**'s offspring have raced in Cheltenham's hurdle events, the obvious reason being that **Galileo** is first and foremost a Flat stallion. Indeed, **Galileo** is one of the world's leading sires, his reputation being bolstered even further during this decade having sired the world renowned *Frankel*. Unbeaten in 14 starts, *Frankel* was rated at 147 by Timeform following his victory in the 2012 *Queen Anne Stakes at Royal Ascot*, making him their highest-rated horse in the organisation's history.

It won't happen that often, but I can well imagine some know-all in one of Cheltenham's Corporate Hospitality boxes announcing that one of the hurdlers in the forthcoming race has been sired by the same stallion that sired *Frankel*, and then the whole group placing their bets on the blue-blooded runner. More often than not, their money will go down the drain, and they will be disappointed. The fact is that the 3 wins and 2 places recorded by **Galileo** bred festival runners, are down to just 3 of the progeny. Moreover, if we exclude the ten festival appearances from these three winners, of the remaining 25 runs at Cheltenham, only five of them have resulted in **Galileo**'s offspring recording a top six finish.

There is no doubt, however, that the odd **Galileo** sired and classy flat-bred will pop up at Cheltenham and win. Three of them have already, two in the past three years. At the 2015 Cheltenham Festival, the *Dermot Weld* trained ***Windsor Park*** (9/2), was entered for the *Neptune Investment Management Novices' Hurdle*, and jockey *Davy Russell* had his mount up with the leaders throughout, before running on well after the last, to win quite comfortably from runner-up *Parlour Games*.

At that same meeting, the five year old, ***Supasundae***, who had only been on a racecourse twice previously, winning both of his National Hunt Flat starts, finished sixth at the festival's *Weatherbys Champion Bumper*. The following year, ***Supasundae***, trained by *Henry De Bromhead*, was somewhat surprisingly, the only one of **Galileo**'s offspring to appear at the 2016 Cheltenham Festival. Running freely in the *Sky Bet Supreme Novices' Hurdle*, ***Supasundae*** raced handily but lacked an extra kick towards the business end of the race and finished in seventh at odds of 12/1. It would appear that the change of scenery from *Henry De Bromhead*'s yard to *Jessica Harrington*'s stable did the trick, as it was third time lucky for ***Supasundae*** supporters last season, when at the rewarding odds of 16/1, ***Supasundae***, contesting only his second handicap, ran on strongly to win the 2017 *Coral Cup Handicap Hurdle*.

Still only eight years old, it will be interesting to see if ***Supasundae*** can stay fit and return to the festival three more times, to match the exertions of the stand out hurdler of **Galileo**'s stock, ***Celestial Halo***. Appearing six times at the Cheltenham Festival, ***Celestial Halo*** rewarded punters with winnings on three occasions. He provided owner *Andy Stewart* with his first ever festival winner by taking the 2008 *JCB Triumph Hurdle*; finished second the following season in the 2009 *Smurfit Kappa Champion Hurdle Challenge Trophy*; and attempting three miles for the first time in the *Ladbrokes World Hurdle* in 2013, at a price of 40/1, he ran another cracking race to finish runner-up to the *Charles Byrnes* trained, *Solwhit*. It is interesting to note that ***Celestial Halo*** had an Official Flat Rating of 110, a figure he obtained when as a three year old, he finished 7th in the 2007 *Ladbrokes St Leger Stakes* at *Doncaster*. It was his last race on the flat, as he was later purchased by *Andy Stewart* and sent to *Paul Nicholls*' yard at *Ditcheat*.

Further analysis shows that the Official Flat Rating of **Galileo**'s progeny is probably the best pointer as to whether they will perform at a Cheltenham Festival. Of the 24 of the progeny to have raced at Cheltenham, 21 of them had an Official Flat Rating, courtesy of them running at least three times on the flat. All 16 of the offspring who could not manage to achieve a top rating of at least 100 during their flat career, have generally struggled at the festival with none of them able to register a top four finish. Of the five who did break the 100 barrier, two of them won at the festival. ***Windsor Park*** achieved a flat rating of 102 from his four runs on the flat, although he kicked off his career with five runs in National Hunt Flat races, and ***Celestial Halo***'s exploits and flat rating of 100 have been highlighted above. The other three of the offspring who were rated above 100 failed to win or place, but on at least one of their festival appearances, all three managed to finish 7th or higher. Just three **Galileo** sired festival runners did not race on the flat, all starting their careers in National Hunt Flat Races, one being recent winner, ***Supasundae***.

In summary, **Galileo** is a superlative stallion of top class flat racehorses, but that does not translate to **Galileo** being a leading Jumps Stallion. The fact is that supporting **Galileo** sired runners at Cheltenham Festivals has been unprofitable. Backing all 35 runners would have resulted in a loss of £20.90 to a £1.00 each-way stake. That said, every now and again, **Galileo**'s offspring do win, as evidenced by ***Supasundae***'s success last year and ***Windsor Park***'s victory in 2015. If you are keen on a **Galileo** bred festival entry, for it to have any chance of winning, make sure your pick has either an Official Flat Rating of 100 plus, or that your selection's career began in National Hunt Flat races. **Galileo**'s offspring that meet neither criterion can be safely disregarded.

Germany (USA)

Quote from the 2017 Cheltenham Festival Stallion Guide - "The 12 festival appearances are down to just five of **Germany**'s progeny, and another exceptional statistic to bear in mind, is that only two of those five have so far failed to win a Cheltenham Festival event."

Germany (Died as a 22-y-o in 2013)							
Race Format	*Miles*	*Won*	*Placed*	*Unplaced*	*Total*	*Win %*	*Place %*
Hurdles	About 2m	2	0	2	4	50%	50%
	About 2m 4f	1	0	0	1	100%	100%
	About 3m	0	0	0	0	-	-
Chases	About 2m	1	1	4	6	17%	33%
	About 2m 4f	0	0	1	1	0%	0%
	About 3m	0	0	0	0	-	-
	About 4m	0	0	0	0	-	-
Bumper	About 2m	0	0	0	0	-	-
Total	**2008-2017**	**4**	**1**	**7**	**12**	**33%**	**42%**

On 2nd April 2016, in an Irish Point to Point meeting at *Monksgrange, County Wexford*, a horse called ***Samcro*** won as the 2/5 favourite over a distance of three miles and in heavy going. Six months later, ***Samcro*** was purchased for £335,000 by *Gigginstown House Stud* and sent to *Gordon Elliott*'s yard. Since then, ***Samcro*** has raced five times under rules, three times in National Hunt Flat races and two runs over hurdles, the last of which (at the time of writing) was in the Grade 3 *"Monksfield" Novice Hurdle* at *Navan* on 26th November 2017. ***Samcro*** has won all five races and has been the odds-on favourite every time. His sire is **Germany**.

Germany's progeny don't appear too often at *Prestbury Park* in March. Indeed, the stallion has only had five of his offspring experience the noise and excitement of Cheltenham Festivals. These five have engaged in a total of just thirteen festival contests, twelve of which have occurred in the past decade. As of January 30th 2018, ***Samcro*** was holding three festival entries; The *Sky Bet Supreme Novices' Hurdle* (2m½f) at a price of around 5/1; The *Albert Bartlett Novices' Hurdle* (3m) at 8/1; and the *Ballymore Novices' Hurdle* (2m5f) at 6/4. Should all be well and he makes it to Cheltenham in March, then he will be the sixth of **Germany**'s progeny to make a festival appearance. I guess there is a chance that he will flop at Cheltenham like the two British trained of **Germany**'s stock; ***Fighting Chance*** and ***Germany Calling***. But I very much doubt it. ***Fighting Chance*** was pulled up in his one run, but he was at a price of 10/1 which is bigger than all three SPs that are currently available for ***Samcro***. As for ***Germany Calling***, he has fallen once at a price of 100/1, and finished 17th on his other two runs when priced at 33/1 and again at 100/1. Like ***Samcro***, the other three of **Germany**'s offspring all hail from Irish yards and all three of them have done rather better. You may have heard of them; ***Tiger Cry*** won once and was placed once from his three festival appearances; ***Captain Cee Bee*** won once and was placed once from his four festival runs; and ***Faugheen*** has appeared twice and won twice. ***Samcro*** is clearly in very good company and his profile is much more in keeping with these three festival winners.

Samcro looks certain to be at this year's Cheltenham Festival and I am keeping my fingers crossed that ***Faugheen*** will also make the trip over to Gloucestershire. ***Faugheen*** has missed the past two festivals due to injuries and although connections are bullish about his participation at the 2018

Cheltenham Festival, I'm not so confident. On 19th November 2017, on his first racecourse appearance for 22 months, all was looking good as he won the *Unibet Morgiana Hurdle* at *Punchestown* in style. But a little over five weeks later, ***Faugheen*** was pulled up and quickly dismounted at *Leopardstown* in the *Ryanair Hurdle*. He was found to be sound after the race and there has been no satisfactory explanation since as to why he performed so poorly. We will learn a lot more if ***Faugheen*** takes his chance in the *BHP Insurance Irish Champion Hurdle* at *Leopardstown* which takes place after this Guide goes to print.

Faugheen's first festival appearance was in the 2014 *Neptune Investment Management Novices' Hurdle* over 2m5f. He was the first of **Germany**'s progeny to run in a festival contest at a distance other than two miles. Not that it mattered. ***Faugheen*** (6/4 favourite) romped to victory under *Ruby Walsh* by 4½ lengths from *Ballyalton*. At the 2015 Cheltenham Festival, ***Faugheen*** was the 4/5 odds on favourite for the *Stan James Champion Hurdle Challenge Trophy*, and he did not disappoint his supporters, quickening away up the Cheltenham Hill to win by 1½ lengths, from stablemates *Arctic Fire* and the eleven year old legend, *Hurricane Fly*.

Faugheen has been very impressive in his two visits to the festival so far, but in my view, now he is ten years old, he will need to be extra special if he is to win either of the races for which he holds an entry at the 2018 Cheltenham Festival. At the time of writing, ***Faugheen*** has two entries this spring; the *Sun Bets Stayers' Hurdle* (10/1); and the *Unibet Champion Hurdle Challenge Trophy* (11/4). If we start with the latter, we have to go back to 1981 to find the last horse older than nine to win this event. *Sea Pigeon* (aged 10) won the *Champion Hurdle* in 1980 and repeated the success as an eleven year old the following year. Only five horses over the age of eight have won this prize since 1951, the most recent being *Hurricane Fly*, aged nine, in 2013. As for the *Stayers' Hurdle*, the last horse older than nine years old to win this event was *Crimson Embers* in 1986. If ***Faugheen*** is at his very best, I can see him getting placed in either contest, but I can't see him winning.

Interestingly, within the 13 festival races in which **Germany** has been represented, on five occasions, the **Germany** sired runner was aged ten or older. The worst performance of the five was ***Fighting Chance*** who was 10 years old when he was pulled up in the 2010 *Johnny Henderson Grand Annual Chase Challenge Cup*. But the other four races resulted in a win, a 3rd and two 5th places. ***Tiger Cry***, trained by *Arthur Moore*, was to appear in the aforementioned *Grand Annual* race three times, and he won the event as a ten year old in 2008, two years after he had finished runner-up. He lined up as an eleven year old in the 2009 renewal and finished in 5th place just a nose away from 4th and another place dividend. Like ***Tiger Cry***, ***Captain Cee Bee*** was also a veteran when he secured his festival fifth place. Incredibly, he was 13 years old when he achieved this, running fantastically well in the 2014 *Stan James Champion Hurdle Challenge Trophy*. He went off at 100/1. Three years earlier, as a youthful 10 year old, he finished 3rd in the 2011 *sportingbet.com Queen Mother Champion Chase*. Owned by *J P McManus*, ***Captain Cee Bee*** ran all his four festival races over the minimum trip of two miles. He claimed victory in his first festival appearance, the *Anglo Irish Bank Supreme Novices' Hurdle* in 2008. Probably his most disappointing run was in 2010 when he finished 8th in the 2010 *Irish Independent Arkle Challenge Trophy Chase*.

Of the five of **Germany**'s progeny to have appeared at a festival, 60% of them (***Tiger Cry***, ***Captain Cee Bee*** and ***Faugheen***) have already won. If trainer *Willie Mullins* is able to get ***Faugheen*** to the 2018 Cheltenham Festival and have him at his best, then I believe he may well succeed in securing a place. But as a ten year old, I can't see him winning. Supporters of **Germany** need not fret. A **Germany** sired runner will win at this year's festival, just not ***Faugheen***. No prizes for guessing my nap of the festival. It is ***Samcro***.

Gold Well (GB)

Quote from the 2017 Cheltenham Festival Stallion Guide - "Taking all 15 runs to date, **Gold Well** supporters have watched the offspring build up a highly impressive Cheltenham Festival record, registering a top six finishing position on two in every three races, and being rewarded with a win or place on six occasions."

Gold Well (17-y-o)							
Race Format	Miles	Won	Placed	Unplaced	Total	Win %	Place %
Hurdles	About 2m	0	0	0	0	-	-
	About 2m 4f	0	1	1	2	0%	50%
	About 3m	1	0	4	5	20%	20%
Chases	About 2m	0	0	0	0	-	-
	About 2m 4f	0	1	3	4	0%	25%
	About 3m	1	2	3	6	17%	50%
	About 4m	0	0	4	4	0%	0%
Bumper	About 2m	0	0	2	2	0%	0%
Total	**2008-2017**	**2**	**4**	**17**	**23**	**9%**	**26%**

There was a big turn-out at the 2017 Cheltenham Festival from **Gold Well**'s stock, where eight of the progeny lined up in five of the 28 festival races. The previous 15 runs at the festival had been highly encouraging with two wins and four places equating to a 40% win and place strike rate, and a profit of £40.25 to a £1.00 each-way stake had one blindly backed all 15 of the offspring's appearances. Indeed, at the previous four festivals between 2013 and 2016, supporting all of **Gold Well**'s representatives blind to level stakes, would have resulted in a profit at three of the four meetings, the exception being in 2015 where backing all five runners at £1.00 each way would have resulted in a small loss of £2.75.

Against the above backdrop, for fans of this stallion, the 2017 Cheltenham Festival turned out to be rather wretched, as none of the eight **Gold Well** sired runners that took part, could manage a place position; let alone win. Perhaps the performance of ***Holywell*** in the *Ultima Handicap Chase*, the third race on the opening day of the festival, was a warning sign. Between 2014 and 2016, this Grade 3 event run over a distance of 3m½f, had resulted in a **Gold Well** sired runner finishing 1st or 2nd in the race. In 2014, at odds of 10/1, ***Holywell*** won this event (then named the *Baylis & Harding Affordable Luxury Handicap Chase)*, beating *Ma Filleule* by 1¾ lengths. In 2015, the *Henry De Bromhead* trained, ***Grand Jesture***, was handed the task of making it two wins in two years for a **Gold Well** sired runner. It was a gallant effort from the 25/1 shot to finish runner-up, but he was always being held by the winner, *The Druids Nephew*. ***Holywell*** was aimed at the race for a second time in 2016, having finished a very respectable 4th in the preceding season's *Betfred Cheltenham Gold Cup Chase*. But like ***Grand Jesture*** before him, he also had to settle for second place, as *Un Temps Pour Tout* won readily by 7 lengths. In the 2017 running of the *Ultima*, ***Holywell*** was to take on *Un Temps Pour Tout* once again, but their performances could not have been wider apart. *Un Temps Pour Tout* went on to win the contest for a second time, whereas, ***Holywell***, now a 10 year old, jumped with no fluency whatsoever and was pulled up half way round.

The following day, on the Wednesday, there were two **Gold Well** sired entries amongst the list of runners for the cross country *Glenfarclas Chase*. I was very surprised at the price of the *Philip Hobbs* trained ***Sausalito Sunrise***. To win this race, ideally one should have already experienced the Cheltenham cross-country course, or at least been engaged in a cross-country chase elsewhere. ***Sausalito Sunrise*** was priced up at odds of 8/1 and yet this was his first experience of cross-country fences. Needless to say, he struggled throughout, never on terms and finished tailed off and lame when passing the post last of the 12 who finished. The other **Gold Well** representative, ***Ballyboker Bridge***, had experienced this course twice before, one of which was at the 2016 Cheltenham Festival where he finished 6th, later promoted to 5th, following the disqualification of the on the day 'winner', *Any Currency*. In the 2017 renewal, it was déjà vu for ***Ballyboker Bridge***(25/1) as once again he came home in 6th position.

Three of the 24 runners that lined up in last year's *Pertemps Network Final Handicap Hurdle*, were sired by **Gold Well**. The 50/1 outsider, ***Arctic Gold*** was up with the leaders until his stamina drained away two out and he finished in 20th. The *Suzy Smith* trained, ***Clondaw Cian*** (16/1), also started to weaken towards the end of the race and came home in 17th position. The best performance from the **Gold Well** sired trio came from ***Sutton Manor***, one of many festival runners owned by *Gigginstown House Stud*. The *Gordon Elliott* trained 16/1 chance just missed out on a place dividend when finishing in fifth.

The other two **Gold Well** bred entries at the 2017 Cheltenham Festival were both big outsiders and finished outside the top ten in their respective races. ***Better Getalong*** (50/1) was one pace when taking 12th position in the *Weatherbys Champion Bumper* and in the *St. James's Place Foxhunter Challenge Cup Open Hunters' Chase*, ***Grand Jesture*** (40/1) finished in 15th.

Before last year, at every festival at which the stallion's stock was represented, a **Gold Well** sired runner had managed to record a top two finish, so all in all, 2017 was clearly disappointing. Nevertheless, taken overall, one would still be £24.25 better off had one placed a £1.00 each-way wager on all 23 of **Gold Well**'s festival runners to date. In my view, it is too early to write off the chances of **Gold Well**'s offspring at the 2018 Cheltenham Festival based upon one poor year out of five. My hunch is that the 2017 festival was a one-off, so don't be put off should one of your fancies be out of **Gold Well**. Go ahead and place your bet.

High Chaparral (IRE)

Quote from the 2017 Cheltenham Festival Stallion Guide - "Considering that 14 of the 17 **High Chaparral** bred festival runners were sent off at odds greater than 20/1, including seven runners considered rank outsiders with an SP of between 50/1 and 200/1, to have a festival record of two victories and a place is admirable."

High Chaparral (Died as a 15-y-o in 2014)							
Race Format	*Miles*	***Won***	***Placed***	***Unplaced***	***Total***	***Win %***	***Place %***
Hurdles	About 2m	2	0	13	15	13%	13%
	About 2m 4f	0	0	1	1	0%	0%
	About 3m	0	0	1	1	0%	0%
Chases	About 2m	1	0	0	1	100%	100%
	About 2m 4f	0	0	0	0	-	-
	About 3m	0	1	2	3	0%	33%
	About 4m	0	0	0	0	-	-
Bumper	About 2m	0	0	1	1	0%	0%
Total	**2008-2017**	**3**	**1**	**18**	**22**	**14%**	**18%**

Of the 16 **High Chaparral** sired horses to have appeared at a Cheltenham Festival, one stands out above all others, the *Nicky Henderson* trained ***Altior***. At the time of writing, ***Altior*** has been engaged in five hurdle races and six chases. He has won all of them. His only defeats were in in two National Hunt Flat Races during the first four months of 2015. His first festival appearance was in the 2016 *Sky Bet Supreme Novices' Hurdle*, where ***Altior*** (4/1) was particularly impressive, quickening clear after the last, to win by seven lengths ahead of the 15/8 favourite, *Min*. That was his last appearance over hurdles as *Nicky Henderson* started the process to campaign ***Altior*** over fences. Following four runs over fences, all of which he won starting as the odds-on favourite, he returned to the Cheltenham Festival in 2017 to line up in the meeting's second event, the *Racing Post Arkle Challenge Trophy Novices' Chase*. There was no great depth to the race as the *Patricia Pugh* owned star had almost certainly scared off a number of other potential entries. Although taking a little while to engage top gear, ***Altior*** stormed up the Cheltenham run-in to beat *Cloudy Dream* by six lengths. He returned the 1/4 odds-on favourite.

A month after his *Arkle* victory, ***Altior*** won at *Sandown* in the *bet365 Celebration Chase* and was due to appear at the course again last December in the *Betfair Tingle Creek Chase*. However, in mid-November, he was found to be making a whistling noise which required a wind operation and hence he was withdrawn from *Sandown*'s feature event. At the time of writing, connections are upbeat about ***Altior***'s well-being and he is on course to appear at the 2018 Cheltenham Festival in the *Betway Queen Mother Champion Chase*.

It is rather fascinating that of the 22 festival appearances of **High Chaparral**'s offspring, 16 of them have come in the festival's juvenile and novice events. Even more intriguing is that only the three runners who finished in the first three positions of these juvenile and novice events, ***Altior***, ***Hawk High*** and ***Hadrian's Approach***, went on to make another appearance at a festival meeting. ***Hawk High*** was a surprise 33/1 winner when winning the 2014 *Fred Winter Juvenile Handicap Hurdle* and he has appeared at every festival since. He finished 20th and 9th in the 2015 and 2016 *Vincent O'Brien County Handicap Hurdle* events before attempting 2m5f for the first time in the *Coral Cup Handicap*

Hurdle in 2017, where he came home in 13th. ***Hadrian's Approach*** was sent off at 7/1 on his festival debut in the 2013 *RSA Chase* securing a third place dividend. The following year, *Nicky Henderson* entered ***Hadrian's Approach*** in the *Baylis & Harding Affordable Luxury Handicap Chase*, and despite being second favourite for the race at a price of 8/1, the bay gelding never troubled the leaders and came home well beaten in 14th. Following a two year absence, sadly the 2017 *Fulke Walwyn Kim Muir Challenge Cup Amateur Riders' Handicap Chase*, was to be the last race in which ***Hadrian's Approach*** would appear. The *Nicky Henderson* trained 10 year old fell at around half-way resulting in a fatal injury. The other novice winner to race again at a festival was *Supreme* winner, ***Altior***, who as previously highlighted, went on to win the *Arkle*. It will be interesting to see if ***Landofhopeandglory*** (8/1) who took 5th place in the 2017 *JCB Triumph Hurdle* and ***Montana Belle*** (100/1) who finished 13th in the 2017 *Trull House Stud Mares' Novices' Hurdle*, follow the historic trend of **High Chaparral**'s progeny of never again to appear at a Cheltenham Festival if failing to record a debut top three spot in a novice or juvenile event.

Of the 16 appearances in novice and juvenile festival contests, it is definitely worth noting that 12 of the **High Chaparral** bred runners lined up at odds of 20/1 or bigger, with seven of the 12 returning prices of between 50/1 and 200/1. The majority of the twelve outsiders finished well down the field, with ***Hawk High***'s aforementioned 33/1 victory in the 2014 *Fred Winter*, being the only result that delivered a return for punters. The 4 runners who went off at single figure odds have all been previously mentioned, but it is interesting to note that they all secured a top five finish; ***Altior***'s two wins at 1/4 odds-on and 4/1; ***Hadrian's Approach*** securing 3rd in the 2013 *RSA Chase*; and ***Landofhopeandglory***'s 5th placing in the 2017 *JCB Triumph Hurdle*.

There have been five festival handicap events in which a **High Chaparral** bred runner has competed, and sifting through the earlier commentary, one can deduce that all five runs have been courtesy of ***Hawk High*** and the ill-fated ***Hadrian's Approach***, with the former's 9th position in the 2015 *County Handicap Hurdle* being the highest placing. To complete the picture, the one other run from the progeny was ***Montana Belle***'s 8th placing in the *Weatherbys Champion Bumper*.

As March 2018 approaches, based upon his two previous festival appearances and providing the wind operation has had no ill-effects, then ***Altior*** is a worthy favourite for the highly anticipated *Betway Queen Mother Champion Chase*. But there are some big guns likely to be in opposition. At the time of writing, entries include *Douvan*, *Min*, *Politologue*, *Un De Sceaux* and *Yorkhill*.

Besides ***Altior***, if the last 22 appearances are anything to go by, then my advice would be to ignore all other **High Chaparral** sired festival entries unless they are towards the front of the market in the juvenile or novice events. Of the four that lined up at single figure odds, two won (both ***Altior***) and the other couple had respectable runs finishing 3rd and 5th. As to the 12 outsiders with SPs of 20/1 or greater in these contests, there could be a surprise of course as evidenced by ***Hawk High***'s 33/1 victory, but two 5th placings aside, nine of the other eleven runners all finished down the field. And based upon five disappointing handicap performances from ***Hawk High*** and ***Hadrian's Approach***, if there are any **High Chaparral** bred entries in the festival's non-juvenile handicaps, my advice is to disregard these too.

Kalanisi (IRE)

Quote from the 2017 Cheltenham Festival Stallion Guide - "I will certainly be very interested in any of the progeny's 2m hurdle runners should the entrant's odds be 14/1 or less. As advised earlier, in previous festivals, six of the seven **Kalanisi** sired runners who had met these criteria finished in the top six places, including 2 winners and 2 places."

Kalanisi (22-y-o)							
Race Format	*Miles*	*Won*	*Placed*	*Unplaced*	*Total*	*Win %*	*Place %*
Hurdles	About 2m	1	2	7	10	10%	30%
	About 2m 4f	0	0	5	5	0%	0%
	About 3m	0	0	2	2	0%	0%
Chases	About 2m	0	0	0	0	-	-
	About 2m 4f	0	0	2	2	0%	0%
	About 3m	0	0	1	1	-	-
	About 4m	0	0	0	0	-	-
Bumper	About 2m	1	0	4	5	20%	20%
Total	**2008-2017**	**2**	**2**	**21**	**25**	**8%**	**16%**

Over 30 years ago, when I was much younger, I remember watching on television what has turned out to be one of my favourite races of all time, the 1986 *Prix de l'Arc de Triomphe*. I can't remember whether I had placed a bet or not, but throughout the race my eyes were peeled on the famous pink, white and green silks of *Khalid Abdullah*, owner of the great *Dancing Brave*. I adored *Dancing Brave* because he possessed an amazing burst of speed usually coming from the back of the field powering past those in front as if they were just running on at the one pace. He failed to win just two of his ten races, one of which was the 1986 *Derby* where he accelerated in the final furlong but failed to catch the leader *Shahrastani*. As they came round the home turn in the *Prix de l'Arc de Triomphe*, I was certain that he couldn't win. *Dancing Brave* had a wall of around a dozen horses in front of him, including top-class performers like *Bering*, *Triptych*, *Shardari* and the Derby winner, *Shahrastani*. With about two furlongs to run, jockey *Pat Eddery* asked him to quicken, and with a sudden devastating surge down the outside of the pack, he won going away by 1½ lengths. To me, there is something very special about a racehorse, or a human athlete for that matter, that can produce a finishing kick and burst of speed at the tail end of a race. When I witness it happen, I become overwhelmed with excitement.

On 15th March 2017, in somewhat different circumstances and in a very dissimilar race, the *Weatherbys Champion Bumper* at Cheltenham, the memories of *Dancing Brave*'s famous *Prix de L'Arc de Triomphe* victory came flooding back. ***Fayonagh***, sired by **Kalanisi**, was just one of two mares to line up in field and for most of the race, she was in last place. With perhaps ½ mile still to go, the mare had managed to pass a few of her competitors, but as they turned for home and the pace started to increase, she still had most of the field in front of her. Unable to see a way past, jockey *Jamie Codd* switched ***Fayonagh*** right and to the outside and started to make headway. With a remarkable turn of foot, the mare, trained by *Gordon Elliott*, flew past all her rivals and won by 1¼ lengths at a price of 7/1.

I was dreadfully sad when I heard that ***Fayonagh*** had lost her life on 25th October 2017. The mare, owned by *Maura Gittins*, was humanely put down having broken her hind leg on the gallops. Within

24 hours of hearing the tragic news, I vowed that the photograph on the front cover of this 2018 Cheltenham Festival Guide would be that of ***Fayonagh*** winning the *Weatherbys Champion Bumper*. Rest in peace, ***Fayonagh***.

There were six **Kalanisi** sired runners at last year's Cheltenham Festival, one of which was entered for the *Stan James Champion Hurdle Challenge Trophy*. There had only been one previous **Kalanisi** bred runner in this prestigious event and that was the *Alan King* trained ***Katchit***, who followed up his 2007 victory in the *JCB Triumph Hurdle* by winning the *Smurfit Kappa Champion Hurdle Challenge Trophy* twelve months later, beating *Osana* by a length. Trainer Alan King was hoping that ***Katchit*** could win a festival race for the third consecutive year, when entering ***Katchit*** for the 2009 renewal of the *Champion*, but the 2008 winner finished in sixth behind winner *Punjabi*, trained by *Nicky Henderson*. **Kalanisi**'s offspring have a very respectable record in the festival's two mile hurdle races, as does trainer *Nicky Henderson*, and hence I was expecting a good performance from the *Nicky Henderson* trained and **Kalanisi** sired 13/2 chance, ***Brain Power***. But it wasn't to be. ***Brain Power*** ran well up to the second last but then emptied quickly, weakening and trailing home some 30 lengths behind the winner. It was still a good race for *Nicky Henderson* however. His other two in the race *Buveur D'Air* and *My Tent Or Yours* finished 1st and 2nd respectively. Before ***Brain Power***'s 8th placing last year, (he was moved up a place from 9th following the disqualification of *Yanworth*), six of the previous seven **Kalanisi** sired runners who started at 14/1 or less in the festival's two mile hurdle events, had finished in the top six places. This includes ***Katchit***'s two victories as well as a 2nd and a 3rd in the 2010 *JCB Triumph Hurdle*, courtesy of ***Barizan*** and ***Alaivan***.

If we include ***Katchit***'s 2007 Triumph Hurdle success, (the first time a **Kalanisi** sired horse had appeared at a Cheltenham Festival), then 16 of the progeny's 26 festival appearances have been run over a distance of two miles. Of the remaining ten festival runs, only on three occasions has a **Kalanisi** bred runner been tried over the bigger obstacles and so far without success. Two of the offspring tackled the Cheltenham fences last year; ***Another Hero*** (9/1) was never in the race when finishing 13th in the *3m Fulke Walwyn Kim Muir Challenge Cup Amateur Riders' Handicap Chase*; and ***Templehills*** (66/1) was pulled up in the 2½m *Close Brothers Novices' Handicap Chase*. On the only other occasion that a **Kalanisi** representative was entered in a festival 2½m chase, the outcome was the same; ***Act Of Kalanisi*** being pulled up in the 2014 *Byrne Group Plate*. The seven runs from the progeny in the festival's longer distance hurdle races have also left a lot to be desired, with just one top six finishing position, this being ***Barters Hill*** 4th place in the 2016 *Albert Bartlett Novices' Hurdle*.

If you are going to support one of **Kalanisi**'s stock at the 2017 Cheltenham Festival, then based upon the statistical trends to date, it would appear that your best chance of making money is by supporting the progeny in the festival's six contests within the 2m hurdle category. Punters may also be interested should any **Kalanisi** sired entry be listed amongst the runners in Wednesday's *Weatherbys Champion Bumper*, but don't expect anything to come from the clouds like last year's winner, ***Fayonagh***.

Kapgarde (FR)

Quote from the 2017 Cheltenham Festival Stallion Guide - "Based on the 23 runs to date, **Kapgarde**'s offspring have landed just two place positions at Cheltenham Festivals, so the early signs are not encouraging."

Kapgarde (19-y-o)							
Race Format	*Miles*	***Won***	***Placed***	***Unplaced***	***Total***	***Win %***	***Place %***
Hurdles	About 2m	0	1	8	9	0%	11%
	About 2m 4f	0	1	3	4	0%	25%
	About 3m	0	0	2	2	0%	0%
Chases	About 2m	0	0	2	2	0%	0%
	About 2m 4f	0	0	6	6	0%	0%
	About 3m	0	0	2	2	0%	0%
	About 4m	0	0	1	1	0%	0%
Bumper	About 2m	0	0	1	1	0%	0%
Total	**2008-2017**	**0**	**2**	**25**	**27**	**0%**	**7%**

In last year's Guide, I advised punters to be wary of placing bets on **Kapgarde**'s offspring and with the highest placing being 8th from last year's four festival representatives, there is no inkling of evidence to alter my opinion. The 8th placing isn't much to write home about either, as it was achieved from a field of just 10 runners in the *Betway Queen Mother Champion Chase*. Disputing the lead early on, ***Garde La Victoire*** (14/1) was soon being pushed along just before half way and was beaten a long way from home.

The **Kapgarde** sired ***Dolos*** (12/1) fared little better when appearing in his 6th race over hurdles, this being the *Fred Winter Juvenile Handicap Hurdle* over 2m½f. In his previous five races, he had always secured a top three finish, but not on this occasion. Despite working his way into the race two hurdles from home, he was soon being ridden by jockey *Sam Twiston-Davies*, and eventually weakened to finish 13th. Arguably, the most promising performance from the progeny was in the 28th race of the festival, the *Johnny Henderson Grand Annual Challenge Cup Handicap Chase*. Rank outsider of the 24 runners was the *Colin Tizzard* trained, ***Ultragold***, nine years old and priced up at 100/1. The gelding was tracking the leaders, made an effort two out before being outpaced and then stayed on up the Cheltenham Hill. Considering the starting price, finishing a little over twelve lengths off the winner in ninth position, was a reasonable effort. The fourth of **Kapgarde**'s runners last year, ***Hammersly Lake***, was also very disappointing, the 16/1 chance being pulled up at half way in the *Close Brothers Novices' Handicap Chase*.

With four more defeats, **Kapgarde**'s offspring have now failed to trouble the judge in 25 of 27 Cheltenham Festival appearances. There are two exceptions, ***Edgardo Sol*** and ***Ubak***, who both managed to secure a place dividend. ***Edgardo Sol*** (25/1) stayed on really strongly in the 2012 *Vincent O'Brien County Handicap Hurdle*, but couldn't quite get up to catch the winner, *Alderwood*, ridden by the vastly experienced top jockey, *A P McCoy*. And four years later, ***Ubak***, at odds of 28/1, had managed to take the lead just before the last in the 2016 *Coral Cup*, but in the end, he had to settle for third spot, staying on at the one pace and being headed up the run in.

With a 7% place strike rate and having yet to provide a winner from 27 festival runs, a £38.75 loss would have been the result if one had placed a £1.00 each-way bet on all of **Kapgarde**'s festival representatives to date. Unless there is a significant positive change in performances, there is one only recommendation to be made. Strike a line through all of **Kapgarde** bred entries who line up at the 2018 Cheltenham Festival.

Kayf Tara (GB)

Quote from the 2017 Cheltenham Festival Stallion Guide - "I am of the opinion that the 2016 Cheltenham Festival will be as good as it gets for **Kayf Tara**, where the progeny secured a victory for one in every 8 runs. Over the past decade, the festival win strike rate is 6%, not last year's 12%, and that equates to losing 15 bets before finding a winner, which in turn means losses rather than profits. For **Kayf Tara** bred runners at the 2017 Cheltenham Festival, by all means, bet on ***Thistlecrack***. As for the rest, strike a line through them."

Kayf Tara (24-y-o)							
Race Format	*Miles*	***Won***	***Placed***	***Unplaced***	***Total***	***Win %***	***Place %***
Hurdles	About 2m	0	0	12	12	0%	0%
	About 2m 4f	0	2	18	20	0%	10%
	About 3m	2	1	16	19	11%	16%
Chases	About 2m	1	3	9	13	8%	31%
	About 2m 4f	0	0	11	11	0%	0%
	About 3m	3	5	15	23	13%	35%
	About 4m	0	1	6	7	0%	14%
Bumper	About 2m	1	0	4	5	20%	20%
Total	**2008-2017**	**7**	**12**	**91**	**110**	**6%**	**17%**

The very first **Kayf Tara** sired runner at a Cheltenham Festival resulted in the *Gary Moore* trained, ***Grasp***, being pulled up before two out, in the 2006 *Fred Winter Juvenile Novices' Handicap Hurdle*. Since that very first run, 65 more of **Kayf Tara**'s progeny have registered 110 appearances between them, all of which have taken place in the past decade. Perhaps the performance of ***Grasp*** was a sign of things to come for **Kayf Tara** bred runners, as the vast majority of the offspring have returned to their stables from the excitement of Prestbury Park, with little reward for their endeavours.

In looking at the festival performance table, the 17% win & place strike rate, which is mediocre at best, is heavily influenced by the performances of just four of those 66 of **Kayf Tara**'s progeny. The four horses are ***Alfie Sherrin***, ***Cantlow***, ***Special Tiara*** and ***The Package***, who together have recorded two-thirds of **Kayf Tara**'s 12 festival places and 43% of the 7 festival wins. And for anyone attempting to make a profit out of backing **Kayf Tara**'s representatives at the 2018 Cheltenham Festival, the crux is to find those select few of the offspring who will perform well at festival meetings. And the best of luck with that exercise!

Hats off to anyone who picked out ***Alfie Sherrin***, at odds of 14/1, when he ran on well, in only his second ever Cheltenham race, to land the 2012 *JLT Specialty Handicap Chase*. Two years previously, on his festival debut as the hot 11/4 favourite, he struggled into 12th place in the 2010 *Pertemps Final*. ***Cantlow*** failed to trouble the judge on his second and third festival appearances, but he finished 3rd on his fourth trip to the Cheltenham Festival last year, when the 9/4 favourite in the *Glenfarclas Cross Country Chase*. On his festival debut, five years earlier, he also finished 3rd, as a seven year old, in the 2012 *Pertemps Final*.

Based upon the achievements of ***Special Tiara*** and ***The Package***, perhaps punters should back **Kayf Tara** bred runners, labelled as 'veterans', who have previously been placed at a Cheltenham Festival. Last year, the 10 year old ***Special Tiara*** lined up in the *Queen Mother Champion Chase* for the 4th year in succession, having managed to take 3rd place in both the 2015 and 2016 renewals. The big disappointment in the race was the performance of the 2/9 favourite, *Douvan*, who was clearly in trouble throughout the race (it later emerged he was lame), which resulted in ***Special Tiara*** being the surprise winner at odds of 11/1.

The Package was just five years old when he kicked off his six festival appearances, being tailed off and eventually pulled up in the 2008 *Coral Cup*. Over the next six years, ***The Package***, owned by the family of the late *David Johnson*, was to appear at Cheltenham on four more occasions and all in the same race, albeit with different sponsors, in which he picked up three place dividends. In 2010, he missed out by a head to finish runner-up to *Chief Dan George* in the *William Hill Trophy Handicap Chase*. Two years later, he finished fourth to ***Alfie Sherrin*** in the *JLT Specialty Handicap Chase* and then in 2014, as an 11 year old, he finished third in the *Baylis & Harding Affordable Luxury Handicap Chase*. In 2015, trainer *David Pipe* decided to try his luck by entering ***The Package*** in the *Fulke Walwyn Kim Muir Challenge Cup Handicap Chase*. There aren't too many twelve year old horses that are victorious at Cheltenham Festivals, but ***The Package*** proved that age is no barrier, especially if you are assisted by the exceptional amateur rider, *Jamie Codd*, who rode the veteran to a comfortable 12 length victory.

I congratulate anyone who managed to pick out any of the three winners highlighted above, especially as the shortest price of the trio was ***The Package*** at odds of 9/1. Only seven of the 66 **Kayf Tara** sired horses that have appeared at Cheltenham Festivals have passed the winning post in 1st place, and none of them have managed to register two or more festival wins, hence the poor win strike-rate for **Kayf Tara**'s progeny, with just seven successes from a total of 111 festival runs. Of the other four **Kayf Tara** bred festival winners, it would have been an astute punter to have selected the *Venetia Williams* trained 16/1 winner of the 2009 *Pertemps Final*, ***Kayf Aramis***. The three shortest priced winners from **Kayf Tara**'s progeny all registered their successes at the 2016 Cheltenham Festival, a meeting that represented quite a turnaround for the stallion, not only in that it doubled the total of three festival wins the offspring had achieved before 2016, but also in that all three wins were attained in prestigious non-handicap Grade 1 races. ***Blaklion***, who was pulled up when struggling through the soft going in the 2015 *Albert Bartlett Novices' Hurdle*, was far happier on the quicker ground of the following year, when in the *RSA Chase*, he ran on strongly to win at odds of 8/1. Having trained the very first Cheltenham Festival Grade 1 victory for ***Kayf Tara***'s offspring, *Nigel Twiston-Davies* repeated the trick just a few hours later, when his ***Ballyandy*** (5/1) was victorious in the Grade 1 *Weatherbys Champion Bumper*, beating the *Willie Mullins* trained *Battleford* (25/1) by just a nose.

Out of all 66 of **Kayf Tara**'s stock to have lined up in a Cheltenham Festival race, without doubt, the horse with the best credentials to win his race was ***Thistlecrack***, who started as the even money favourite in the 2016 *Ryanair World Hurdle*. It turned out to be a facile victory for ***Thistlecrack*** who was far better than the rest of the field and he won effortlessly. At the end of 2016, it was no surprise to see trainer *Colin Tizzard* divert ***Thistlecrack*** to race over fences, and after his awe-inspiring performance and annihilation of stablemate *Cue Card* and three other rivals to win the *32Red King George VI Chase* at Kempton Park on Boxing Day 2016, his *Gold Cup* odds were slashed to odds-on. Despite being the favourite for the race, history has repeatedly shown us that Cheltenham's biggest prize is a very hard race for a novice chaser to win. And ***Thistlecrack*** was still a novice. Before *Coneygree*'s victory in the 2015 *Betfred Cheltenham Gold Cup*, the last time that a novice had won a *Gold Cup* was when *Captain Christy*, ridden by *Bobby Beasley*, triumphed in 1974. Sadly, we were denied the chance to see if ***Thistlecrack*** could become the second novice chaser to win the *Gold Cup* in the space of three years, when it was announced just a few weeks before the festival that the horse had suffered a tendon injury which would result in him missing the rest of the season.

Having been off the racecourse for a little over ten months, ***Thistlecrack*** returned to action at *Newbury* in the *Ladbrokes Long Distance Hurdle* on 1st December 2017. Despite being the 11/10 favourite, it was a disappointing run, as the **Kayf Tara** sired gelding emptied quickly two out, having previously travelled well through the race, to finish 5th of six runners. Just over three weeks later, he finished 4th in the *32Red King George VI Chase*, a rather different performance to what we had witnessed in *Kempton*'s showpiece event twelve months earlier. Unfortunately, it would appear that ***Thistlecrack***'s chance of winning a *Cheltenham Gold Cup* is now over. After returning stiff following his run at *Kempton*, a bone scan revealed that the horse had a small stress fracture resulting in him being withdrawn from the *Gold Cup* for a second successive year.

At the 2018 Cheltenham Festival, in all likelihood, there will be somewhere in the region of twenty runners representing **Kayf Tara**. As mentioned earlier, picking out which one, if any, will claim a victory, will be extremely difficult, which is why I typically ignore **Kayf Tara**'s offspring at every Cheltenham Festival. If I was forced to advise punters where to look for a **Kayf Tara** bred festival winner, I would point them in the direction of the last race on Thursday, the *Fulke Walwyn Kim Muir Challenge Cup Handicap Steeple Chase*. **Kayf Tara**'s offspring have lined up in the *Kim Muir* on just four occasions, and three of those appearances have resulted in a profitable return for anyone who had backed the runners each way. A year after his victory in the *JLT Specialty Handicap Chase*, trainer *Jonjo O'Neill* entered the *John P McManus* owned, ***Alfie Sherrin***, in the 2013 renewal of the *Kim Muir*. He finished a well beaten 4th in the race. Two years later, and as highlighted previously, connections were celebrating the victory of ***The Package***. And the third of **Kayf Tara**'s progeny to put up a successful performance in the *Kim Muir* occurred last year, as ***Premier Bond*** stayed on to claim 3rd position behind runner-up and top weight, *Pendra*, who was headed at the finish by the rallying *Domesday Book*, who took the race at the rewarding price of 40/1. Coincidentally, ***Alfie Sherrin***, ***The Package*** and ***Premier Bond*** all had an SP of 9/1! The one and only **Kayf Tara** sired failure in the race was the 66/1 outsider, ***Ballyoliver***, who finished 11th in the 2015 renewal, won by ***The Package***.

In the table that highlights the festival performances and statistics of **Kayf Tara**'s stock, it is clear that the best strike rate is in the 3m chase category, but it is ***The Package*** (1 win, 3 places) and ***Alfie Sherrin*** (1 win, 2 places) who are largely responsible for these figures. Similarly, ***Special Tiara***'s victory and two placings in the *Queen Mother Champion Chase* have a very significant impact on the strike rates within the two mile chase category. Personally, I would forget any thought of a **Kayf Tara** bred winner popping up in a 2m or 2½m event over obstacles. Take out ***Special Tiara***, and in 53 attempts in the festival's hurdle and chase contests run over any distance other than the 3m and 4m categories, **Kayf Tara**'s offspring have only managed to register a top three placing twice, the last of which occurred in 2009 when ***Planet Of Sound*** finished 3rd in the *Irish Independent Arkle Challenge Trophy Chase*. One year earlier, in 2008, ***Venalmar*** was narrowly beaten into 2nd place by *Fiveforthree*, in the *Ballymore Properties Novices' Hurdle*, run over a distance of 2m4½f. The next best performance out of these 53 appearances from **Kayf Tara**'s offspring was ***Michael Flips*** in the 2010 *Coral Cup*, where his 4th place finish provided punters with a place dividend.

Those who have read the three previous editions of this Guide know that I am not a fan of supporting **Kayf Tara**'s progeny at the Cheltenham Festival. And it shouldn't be a surprise when one considers that backing blind every single festival appearance by a **Kayf Tara** bred runner would have resulted in a loss of £85.68 to a £1.00 each-way stake. Even in 2016, when **Kayf Tara**'s offspring registered three victories, anyone who had placed a £1.00 each-way stake on all 25 of **Kayf Tara** sired runners at that meeting, would have made a £23.00 loss. Perhaps one of the offspring will win at the 2018 Cheltenham Festival, but my advice to punters is not to waste your time trying to work out which one it will be from the likely 15-25 **Kayf Tara** bred entries. Focus your efforts to pick winners elsewhere.

King's Theatre (IRE)

Quote from the 2017 Cheltenham Festival Stallion Guide - "One may consider backing every **King's Theatre** sired horse that runs at the 2017 festival, a strategy which over the past 10 years would have delivered a total profit of £14.88 to a £1.00 win stake. This profit, however, is largely due to ***Cue Card's*** 40/1 success in the 2010 *Weatherbys Champion Bumper*. Indeed, adopting this approach over the past 4 years would have resulted in a loss every year and we need to go back to 2012 to find the last time a profit was made."

King's Theatre (Died as a 20-y-o in 2011)							
Race Format	*Miles*	***Won***	***Placed***	***Unplaced***	***Total***	***Win %***	***Place %***
Hurdles	About 2m	1	4	11	16	6%	31%
	About 2m 4f	3	2	23	28	11%	18%
	About 3m	2	3	13	18	11%	28%
Chases	About 2m	1	2	6	9	11%	33%
	About 2m 4f	2	2	15	19	11%	21%
	About 3m	2	3	30	35	6%	14%
	About 4m	2	0	8	10	20%	20%
Bumper	About 2m	1	2	7	10	10%	30%
Total	**2008-2017**	**14**	**18**	**113**	**145**	**10%**	**22%**

Just before the 2017 Cheltenham Festival took place, I read an article by the Bloodstock Editor of the Racing Post, *Martin Stevens*, which was entitled "Why Theatre is king of the sires at Cheltenham". The statement was easily justified as **King's Theatre**'s offspring had recorded ten Cheltenham Festival winners between 2012 and 2016, thereby registering more festival winners than any other jumps stallion over the previous five years. In the article, there was a quote from *John O'Connor*, the Ballylinch Stud Managing Director, who had looked after **King's Theatre** for 15 years. In responding to a request for a festival fancy, he is said to have replied, "The best advice I can give anyone betting at Cheltenham is to follow **King's Theatre**."

Despite recording most winners between 2012 and 2016, with a win strike of 10%, those ten winners came from a total of 97 entries from the progeny over that five year period, and in **King's Theatre**'s case, betting £1.00 each way on all 97 runners would have resulted in making a loss of £46.04. Indeed, we need to go back to 2012 to find the last time a profit was made, when three victories from the 16 **King's Theatre** bred runners would have recorded a profit of just 77p to a £1.00 each-way stake. Unfortunately, at last year's Cheltenham Festival, following the above quoted advice of *Mr O'Connor* would have been rather painful, as all 24 of **King's Theatre** bred runners that appeared at the 2017 Cheltenham Festival were beaten. The last time that **Kings' Theatre** had failed to have a festival winner was back in 2008, when only three of the offspring took part.

There were only two performances of note for **King's Theatre**'s offspring last year, the first of which was in the *RSA Novices Chase*, where ***Bellshill*** stayed on at one pace to finish 3rd and some ten lengths adrift of the dramatics ahead, concerning the *Nicky Henderson* trained pair of *Might Bite* and *Whisper*. *Might Bite* had appeared to have thrown the race away, hanging violently to the stands' side, before rallying to beat *Whisper* by a nose. Probably the best performance from a **King's Theatre** representative at the 2017 Cheltenham Festival, occurred two days later, in the *Randox Health County Handicap Hurdle*, where *Nicky Henderson* witnessed another exciting finish when his **King's**

Theatre sired, ***L'Ami Serge*** at 25/1, finished 2nd and failed by just a neck to reel in the winner, *Arctic Fire*.

It is worth noting that ***L'Ami Serge*** has a good record at the Cheltenham Festival finishing in the first four places on all three of his outings to date. Previous to his runner up spot last season, he finished 3rd in the 2016 *JLT Novices Chase*, and in 2015, he just missed out on a place when finishing 4th in the *Sky Bet Supreme Novices Hurdle*. At the time of writing, ***L'Ami Serge*** currently holds a 2018 Cheltenham Festival entry in the 2018 *Sun Bets Stayers' Hurdle*, and based upon his performances to date and the track record of **King's Theatre**'s offspring in the festival's 3m hurdle events, I consider the gelding has a good each-way chance. In total, there have been 19 **King's Theatre** sired runners who have taken part in festival hurdle races over a distance of three miles, the first of which took place just over a decade ago, when the 11/8 favourite, ***Wichita Lineman*** benefitted from the last hurdle fall of his closest pursuer, *Black Harry*, before going on to win the *Spa Novices' Hurdle* by 12 lengths. Since then, **King's Theatre**'s progeny have registered three runner-up positions and two further victories over the 3m distance. It is worth noting that 7 of the 19 runners that lined up in these events went off at 33/1 or bigger, the best performance of which was ***The Druids Nephew*** who finished 6th at 100/1 in the 2012 *Spa Novices' Hurdle*. Six of the remaining dozen, therefore, who were more fancied in the market at 20/1 or less, have managed to register a win or 2nd placing. For the record, a £1.00 each-way bet on all twelve **King's Theatre** bred runners in the festival's three mile hurdle events, who had an SP of 20/1 or under, would have produced a profit of £10.58.

As well as taking note of the more fancied runners in the festival's long distance hurdle races, punters should also look out for **King's Theatre** bred runners that fall within the festival's two mile hurdle category. Over the past ten years, the progeny have been represented in these events on sixteen occasions, and placing a £1.00 each-way wager on all sixteen runners would have resulted in a profit of £5.37. And typically, punters will at least get a run for their money, as 12 of the 16 contenders finished in the top six places, although only five bets would have resulted in a pay-out. Come the 2018 Cheltenham Festival, if one is interested in a **King's Theatre** bred runner in a two mile hurdle race, then it is advisable to make sure the bet is each way, as the offspring have actually only managed to pass the winning post in first place just the once, when ***Menorah*** was victorious in the 2010 *Supreme Novices Hurdle*. ***Menorah***'s 12/1 victory is clearly a significant contribution to the profit figure highlighted above, as is the runner-up performances of ***Fethard Player*** (33/1) and ***L'Ami Serge*** (25/1) in the past two renewals of the *County Handicap Hurdle*.

To complete the picture over hurdles, when it comes to the 2½ mile category, performances have been largely uninspiring. Over the past decade, eleven of **King's Theatre**'s offspring have taken part in the two 2½m handicap hurdles at the festival, these being the *Coral Cup* and the *Martin Pipe Conditional Jockeys' Handicap Hurdle*. Nine of the eleven runners weren't able to finish higher than 9th position, and so it was rather out of the blue when the *Gordon Elliott* trained, ***Diamond King*** bucked the trend to secure victory in the 2016 *Coral Cup*. Although the progeny have performed better in the non-handicap 2½m hurdle contests, the statistics are still not persuasive enough for me to recommend them in these contests. No conclusions can be drawn from the one and only appearance by a **King's Theatre** bred horse in the *Baring Bingham Novices' Hurdle*, which resulted in victory for ***The New One***. In 2013, with the race being sponsored by *Neptune Investment Management*, ***The New One*** (7/2) ran on strongly to beat *Rule The World*, who himself went on to win the 2016 *Crabbie's Grand National Chase* at *Aintree*.

The other 2½m non-handicap hurdle at the Cheltenham Festival is restricted to mares, the *OLBG Mares' Hurdle*, where **King's Theatre**'s offspring have been represented on no less than sixteen occasions. Only six of the runners lined up at odds of 25/1 or less and, in chronological order, the finishing positions and the starting prices were 5th (9/2), 3rd (9/4), 7th (8/1), 2nd (14/1), 1st (6/1) and 4th

(25/1). In hindsight, supporting all six to a £1.00 each-way stake would have produced a profit of £2.45. Nevertheless, I am not overly enthusiastic about following **King's Theatre**'s stock in the 2018 *OLBG Mares' Hurdle*, as although there is usually a fairly large field in the race, there is little depth and plenty of the contenders have little chance. Since the very first running, in 2008, which was won by *Whiteoak*, there have been three top-class mares outclassing the field, all of whom were trained by *Willie Mullins*. The brilliant *Quevega* won six times between 2009 and 2014, before everyone expected *Annie Power* to outclass the field and be victorious in 2015, only for that infamous last flight fall which destroyed an opening day *Willie Mullins* four-timer and where bookies averted what William Hill called "Armageddon Tuesday." Next to appear was *Vroum Vroum Mag*, who was a class apart when comfortably winning the 2016 renewal as the 4/6 odds on favourite. By far the strongest renewal of the race took place at last year's festival, where the race was contended by three top-notch mares, *Apple's Jade*, *Vroum Vroum Mag* and *Limini*, who predictably filled the front three positions with what turned out to be a thrilling finish.

Referring back to the £2.45 profit highlighted above for **King's Theatre** bred runners lining up at 25/1 or less in this mares contest, it should be noted that the profit is largely due to the **King's Theatre** sired, ***Glens Melody***, benefitting from *Annie Power*'s fall in 2015. In conclusion, this race is won by mares who are a class apart from the rest of the field, so unless **King's Theatre** is represented in the race by one of the top-notch favourites, then my advice to **King's Theatre** fans is to leave the race alone.

At the last 10 Cheltenham Festivals, 85 of **King's Theatre**'s progeny have registered 145 runs between them. Three of the offspring have won at the festival twice, these being ***Balthazar King*** and ***Cue Card*** within the past decade, and ***Wichita Lineman*** whose first win came eleven years ago. I remember ***Wichita Lineman***'s second festival win in the 2009 3m½f *National Hunt Handicap Chase* rather well, not only because of the remarkable ride by *AP McCoy* which many racing fans believe to have been his best ever ride, but because I had backed the horse that had kicked clear on the run-in to the last, looking every bit the most likeliest winner. My money went down the pan as *Mr McCoy* refused to settle for 2nd place and pushed ***Wichita Lineman*** to beat my fancy, *Maljimar*, by a neck. On Betfair, *Maljimar* had traded at an in-running low of 1.06! Six years went past before we would witness a second three mile chase win for **King's Theatre**'s offspring, and it occurred in the 2015 renewal of the event that had been won by ***Wichita Lineman*** in 2009. Now named the *Ultima Business Solutions Handicap Chase,* the victor was ***The Druids Nephew***, trained by *Neil Mulholland* and ridden by *Barry Geraghty,* who rode the 8/1 chance to a relatively comfortable victory, beating *Grand Jesture* by 3¾ lengths. The statistics in the table inform us that the least impressive set of results for **King's Theatre**'s stock are in the three mile chase category. The 6% win strike rate and 14% win & place strike rate are the lowest within the seven race categories, and backing all 35 of **King's Theatre** bred runners in the 3m chase category to a £1.00 each-way stake would have resulted in a loss of £41.25.

As advised earlier, ***Cue Card***, trained by Dorset based *Colin Tizzard*, has also won twice at the Festival, securing victory in the 2013 *Ryanair Chase* three years after his 40/1 trouncing of the opposition in the 2010 *Weatherbys Champion Bumper*. At the last two Cheltenham Festivals, ***Cue Card***, who is probably the most renowned of **King's Theatre**'s offspring, has attempted to win the *Timico Cheltenham Gold Cup Chase*, but on both occasions, he hasn't managed to complete the course, crashing out at the third from home in both renewals. ***Cue Card***'s win in the *Ryanair Chase*, resulted in a **King's Theatre** sired victory in this particular contest for two years running, as in the 2012 renewal, *Barry Geraghty* rode ***Riverside Theatre*** to just get up in the last 50 yards to beat *Albertas Run*. And these two *Ryanair* successes by ***Cue Card*** and ***Riverside Theatre*** are the only two wins for **King's Theatre**'s stock in the festival's 2½ mile chase category. In the past decade, there have been seventeen other attempts by **King's Theatre** bred participants to add to these two victories, but without success. Indeed, the most likely outcome in backing **King's Theatre**'s progeny in 2½ mile chases at the festival is for the horse to be pulled up, which has happened on eight occasions. Even though the offspring have a better win and win/place strike rate in the 2½m chase category, compared to those achieved over three miles, the figures still don't support a case to back **King's Theatre** sired runners in 2½ mile chase events. If one had backed blind all 19 runs in the past decade, the outcome would have been a loss of £18.90 to a £1.00 each-way stake.

If there is an argument to support **King's Theatre**'s stock over the bigger obstacles, then it is in the shortest distance of two miles, where a £1.00 each-way bet on all nine runners, would have provided a tiny profit of £1.10. Five of the nine runs took place in the *Arkle*, the first of which was in 2010, when ***Riverside Theatre*** finished fifth. The following year, the *Philip Hobbs'* trained ***Captain Chris*** at 6/1 finished strongly to win from *Finian's Rainbow*. In 2012, the incredibly impressive *Sprinter Sacre* was in no danger of being beaten, but it was the two **King's Theatre** sired runners who followed him home in 2nd and 3rd, ***Cue Card*** and ***Menorah*** respectively. *Nicky Henderson* had another "sure thing" in 2013 with *Simonsig,* who like *Sprinter Sacre* started at odds-on. Although blundering at the 9th, *Simonsig* went on to win the race from another of **King's Theatre**'s progeny, the 33/1 shot, ***Baily Green***. So, in that four year period of *Arkle* renewals between 2010 and 2013, we have witnessed **King's Theatre** offspring with very impressive finishing positions of first, runner-up twice, third and fifth. It has now been four years in a row for **King's Theatre**'s offspring to be unrepresented in the *Arkle*, but if the progeny do have a runner in the 2018 running, then the trends suggest we should take note.

Although the progeny have recorded two victories in the four mile chase category, they were both courtesy of ***Balthazar King***, who won the *Glenfarclas Cross Country Handicap Chase* twice, in 2012 and 2014. The other eight runs in these long distance chase events are rather inconclusive in terms of determining any meaningful trends for **King's Theatre**'s offspring.

Fans of **King's Theatre** have had a rather ghastly time of it over the past two years, with just the one victory from ***Diamond King*** in the 2016 *Coral Cup*, to show for the 48 of the progeny who have lined up in the 2016 and 2017 Cheltenham Festivals. That said, historically, the offspring typically achieve between one and three winners at every festival, as highlighted by the twelve winners sired by **King's Theatre** during the six year period between 2010 and 2015. Nevertheless, those 12 victories were forthcoming from a total of 92 appearances from the progeny, and if we add in the 48 runs in the past two years, that is a total of 13 victories from 140 attempts. In all likelihood, we will witness a further twenty or more **King's Theatre** bred runners at the 2018 Cheltenham Festival, and in all probability, one or two more festival wins will be added to the offspring's roll of honour. The problem for punters is that backing all the runners blind will probably result in a loss, as only three of the 14 victories within the past decade have been won by horses lining up at double figure odds – with two 12/1 chances and ***Cue Card***'s 40/1 success in the 2010 *Weatherbys Champion Bumper*. The challenge is trying to figure out which one or two of the twenty plus runners will win, and to that end, punters may want to skim through the runners for the festival's 2m hurdle races and also the second race of the four day meeting, the *Racing Post Arkle Challenge Trophy Steeple Chase*. Most attention, however, should be reserved for the festival's three mile hurdle contests as the trends suggest that this is the category where punters are most likely to be rewarded. At the time of writing, two of **King's Theatre**'s progeny are holding entries in the *Sun Bets Stayers' Hurdle*, and I have already advised that I consider ***L'Ami Serge*** to be a sound each-way bet. I am less excited about the chances of the other entry, ***The New One***, who if he takes his chance, will be competing as a 10 year old. The fact is that none of the fifty horses aged 10 or older that have competed in this event in the past 31 renewals have been able to win. The last veteran to win this championship race was *Crimson Embers* in 1986.

Martaline (GB)

Martaline was not featured in the 2017 Cheltenham Festival Stallion Guide.

Martaline (19-y-o)								
Race Format	*Miles*	***Won***	***Placed***	***Unplaced***	***Total***	***Win %***	***Place %***
Hurdles	About 2m	0	0	3	3	0%	0%
	About 2m 4f	0	0	3	3	0%	0%
	About 3m	1	0	5	6	17%	17%
Chases	About 2m	0	0	1	1	0%	0%
	About 2m 4f	1	2	1	4	25%	75%
	About 3m	0	0	3	3	0%	0%
	About 4m	0	0	1	1	0%	0%
Bumper	About 2m	0	1	3	4	0%	25%
Total	**2008-2017**	**2**	**3**	**20**	**25**	**8%**	**20%**

Without deeper analysis, anyone looking at the table above may decide to leave **Martaline**'s progeny alone, unless there is an entry in the festival's 2½m chases. With this stallion, that may well be the best strategy. I don't have an alternative approach, other than perhaps ignoring **Martaline**'s stock entirely, but don't be surprised if a **Martaline** sired runner picks up a festival event in one of the other race categories. Picking out any sort of trend for **Martaline**'s offspring based on previous festival appearances is rather difficult, but I felt that the stallion needed to be included in the Guide this year as the number of festival entries bred by this sire is increasing.

Let's start with the 2½m chase category. Only four runs on the board maybe, but one victory and two places represents a 75% win and place strike rate. Three of those runs, however, came from the *David Pipe* trained ***Dynaste***, the highest rated of **Martaline**'s progeny. In the *Jewson Novices' Chase* in 2013, he went off the 11/8 favourite when finishing runner-up to *Benefficient* who ran on well after the last to win by a healthy 3¼ lengths. The following year, ***Dynaste*** (3/1 favourite) went one better in the 2014 *Ryanair Chase*, quickening two out and then staying on strongly after the last to win by 2¼ lengths from *Hidden Cyclone*. Having missed the 2015 festival with an injury, ***Dynaste*** returned to the festival in 2016, but now running in the *Ryanair Chase* as a ten year old, he didn't have the pace of his younger rivals and came home in 7th place, reflecting his 20/1 odds.

The one other runner sired by **Martaline** to race in a 2½m festival chase is the *Noel Meade* trained ***Disko***, who last season contested the *JLT Novices' Chase* finishing 3rd at 4/1, behind the very impressive *Yorkhill*. Looking at ***Disko***'s entries for the 2018 Cheltenham Festival, he could follow the same route as ***Dynaste*** and head for the *Ryanair Chase* or be diverted to run in the *Timico Cheltenham Gold Cup Chase*. If *Noel Meade* is interested to know how **Martaline**'s offspring have performed in the festival's three mile chases, I can advise that all three attempts in this category happened at last year's festival and none of the three managed to get home. ***Squouateur*** was well fancied for the *Fulke Walwyn Kim Muir Challenge Cup Amateur Riders' Handicap Chase* and started as the 5/1 favourite. He was still quite a long way back when starting to make his move, but made a mistake and unseated his rider, *Jamie Codd*, three fences from home. The other two **Martaline** bred chasers were 33/1 and 100/1 outsiders in their respective races and both were pulled up.

The other four festival runs from **Martaline**'s progeny last year also left a lot to be desired. ***Baden*** (100/1) was last of the 11 finishers in the *Albert Bartlett Novices' Hurdle*; ***Agrapart*** (66/1) was also last of the finishers when 9th in the *Sun Bets Stayers' Hurdle*; ***Poker Play*** (16/1) weakened to register a 14th place finish in the *Fred Winter Juvenile Handicap Hurdle*; and the well fancied ***Carter McKay*** (11/2) finished 15th in the *Weatherbys Champion Bumper*.

Looking at all 25 festival performances from **Martaline**'s offspring, it is interesting to note that apart from the aforementioned performances of ***Dynaste*** and ***Disko*** in the 2½m chase category, there are only two other performances of note. ***Very Wood***'s 33/1 victory in the 2014 *Albert Bartlett Novices' Hurdle*, followed on from ***Dynaste***'s win earlier in the week. They were the only two **Martaline** sired runners to compete at the 2014 festival meeting and produced a 135/1 double. The only other horse worth a mention sired by **Martaline** is the *Willie Mullins* trained ***Pique Sous***, who was ridden into 3rd place by jockey *Ruby Walsh* in the 2012 *Weatherbys Champion Bumper* to finish 1½ lengths behind stablemate *Champagne Fever*. The following season, both the winner and ***Pique Sous*** were entered in the festival's opening race, the *William Hill Supreme Novices' Hurdle* and once again ***Pique Sous*** finished behind his stablemate. With *Ruby Walsh* now aboard, *Champagne Fever* won the race by half a length from *My Tent Or Yours*, with ***Pique Sous*** finishing in 6th place some 23 lengths behind.

In summary, both ***Very Wood*** and ***Dynaste*** have had a significant impact on the overall festival statistics of this stallion. Betting blind to level stakes on all 25 festival appearances of **Martaline**'s offspring has been profitable (a profit of £3.68 to a £1.00 each-way stake). But let's not fool ourselves. Without ***Very Wood***'s 33/1 success in the 2014 *Albert Bartlett Novices' Hurdle*, we would be facing significant losses. And ***Dynaste*** is largely responsible for the positive results in the 2½m chase category.

Bearing the above in mind, what advice can be provided as we approach the 2018 Cheltenham Festival? If you have carried out your analysis of the form and other factors, and have decided on a selection sired by **Martaline**, then you should probably back your judgement, as there is a large chunk of unpredictability about this stallion's runners. And if your selection happens to be running in a 2½m chase around Prestbury Park, then even better, as I have a hunch that **Martaline**'s offspring are most suited to this race discipline. That said, be mindful that of the 18 of the progeny to appear at a Cheltenham Festival, 14 of them have failed to register a top six finish, the exceptions being ***Disko***, ***Dynaste***, ***Pique Sous*** and ***Very Wood***. Go easy!

Midnight Legend (GB)

Quote from the 2017 Cheltenham Festival Stallion Guide - "If you are a Cheltenham Festival devotee who likes to back a horse each way at big prices, then my advice is to look down the list of runners for each day of the festival, and if you happen to come across a horse that has **Midnight Legend** listed as the sire, then put your each-way bet on. The trends suggest that you will get a run for your money fifty percent of the time, and for one in every four bets, you can collect some winnings."

Midnight Legend (Died as a 25-y-o in 2016)							
Race Format	*Miles*	*Won*	*Placed*	*Unplaced*	*Total*	*Win %*	*Place %*
Hurdles	About 2m	0	3	2	5	0%	60%
	About 2m 4f	0	2	10	12	0%	17%
	About 3m	0	0	3	3	0%	0%
Chases	About 2m	0	2	4	6	0%	33%
	About 2m 4f	1	1	8	10	10%	20%
	About 3m	1	1	7	9	11%	22%
	About 4m	1	0	3	4	25%	25%
Bumper	About 2m	0	1	1	2	0%	50%
Total	**2008-2017**	**3**	**10**	**38**	**51**	**6%**	**25%**

The 2017 Cheltenham Festival represented another good year for the stock of **Midnight Legend**. In previous Stallion Guides, I have highlighted that roughly 50% of **Midnight Legend** bred festival runners achieve a top six placing and from the eight of the offspring that lined up at the festival last year, guess how many registered a first six finishing position? Four! And as highlighted in the quote at the top of the page, based on historic trends from festival meetings, one can expect to receive winnings for one in every 4 bets. Well, the results were even better for the progeny in 2017, with a victory and two places from the eight festival appearances, the highlight, of course, ***Sizing John***'s *Gold Cup* triumph.

It is very easy to support **Midnight Legend**'s offspring at Cheltenham Festivals, as one doesn't need to be particularly selective as to the runner's festival track record, the race conditions or the odds on offer. Punters can pretty much back **Midnight Legend**'s progeny blindly; whatever the horse, whatever the race and whatever the odds on offer. Perhaps this needs further explanation. There have been 54 appearances of **Midnight Legend** bred runners at festival meetings, with all bar three of those runs occurring within the past decade. Taking all 54 runs into account, the three victories and eleven place positions have been achieved by eleven different horses, meaning that the offspring's successes are not a reflection of the dominance of just one or two of the offspring. And it doesn't seem to matter to **Midnight Legend**'s stock whether the race is over hurdles or fences, or indeed any specific distance. The win and place positions of **Midnight Legend** bred runners have occurred over fences and hurdles and over distances ranging between two and four miles. Before last year's festival meeting, perhaps one could have argued that **Midnight Legend**'s progeny had never recorded a festival win or place in the three mile chase. Even then, the offspring weren't far off, recording finishing places of between 5th and 7th on five occasions from the seven runs within this category. Following ***Sizing John***'s victory in the 2017 *Timico Cheltenham Gold Cup Chase* and ***Potters Legend*** placing in last year's *Fulke Walwyn Kim Muir Challenge Cup Amateur Riders' Handicap Chase*, **Midnight Legend**'s runners have now recorded a win or place across all the table's race categories. (For the eagle-eyed, the 3m hurdle category does not show ***Itsa Legend***'s 3rd place in the *Brit Insurance Novices' Hurdle*, as this occurred over a decade ago in 2007). And when it comes to the market, should punters only be concerned with those **Midnight Legend** sired runners that are towards the front of the market? The answer is a resounding no! Eight of the fourteen win and place positions have been at odds of 20/1 or far greater. For the record, the odds returned on all 14 win and place positions have been 3/1 fav, 4/1, 7/1, 8/1, 9/1, 10/1, 20/1, 25/1, 25/1, 25/1, 25/1, 50/1, 100/1, 100/1.

Considering that the festival win rate of **Midnight Legend** bred runners is once in every 16 plus appearances (6%), it is perhaps surprising that had one backed blind all 54 festival appearances of **Midnight Legend**'s offspring to a £1.00 each-way stake, the outcome would have been a profit of £39.35. When it comes to this stallion, it is clearly imperative to back the progeny each way, as once in every five festival runs, a **Midnight Legend** runner produces a place dividend, and very often at huge odds.

As referenced above, festival victories are a relatively rare occurrence for **Midnight Legend**'s stock. And a quirky pattern is beginning to emerge of the offspring producing a festival winner every three years! In 2011, ***Holmwood Legend*** was victorious in the Grade 3 *Byrne Group Plate* beating another **Midnight Legend** bred 25/1 shot, ***Aimagayle***, to produce a whopping tote exacta dividend for this sire's supporters of £977.70! Move forward three years and ***Midnight Prayer*** (8/1) just held on from the staying on *Shotgun Paddy* to win, by a neck, the listed 2014 *Terry Biddlecombe National Hunt Chase Amateur Riders' Novices' Chase*. And in 2017, the victory of ***Sizing John*** in the most prestigious prize of all, the *Timico Cheltenham Gold Cup Chase*, may well have brought a tear to the eyes of *David* and *Kathleen Holmes*. The couple purchased **Midnight Legend** in 2001 to stand at their *Pitchall Farm Stud* in *Stratford-upon-Avon*, the stallion covering mares for 15 years before sadly being put down in July 2016.

The build-up in the weeks before the *Timico Cheltenham Gold Cup Chase* had been somewhat noteworthy because of the number of withdrawals from leading fancies, such as *Coneygree*, *Don Cossack*, *Thistlecrack* and *Vautour*. Nevertheless, ***Sizing John*** would line up against some impressive competitors including *Cue Card*, *Djakadam* and *Native River*. ***Sizing John*** was attempting three miles for only the second time in his career. His first run over the distance a month earlier had worked out rather well, when he won the *Stan James Irish Gold Cup Chase* at *Leopardstown* from *Empire Of Dirt*.

As they set off in the *Cheltenham Gold Cup*, jockey *Robbie Power* settled ***Sizing John*** in mid-division with a patient ride, before making headway on the seven year old four fences from home. ***Sizing John*** found plenty of stamina two from home, running on strongly up the hill to beat the staying-on *Minella Rocco* by two and three-quarter lengths. It was a first *Cheltenham Gold Cup* victory for trainer *Jessica Harrington* from her very first runner in the race, an admirable achievement considering that she had been training the horse at her *County Kildare* stables for under a year, owing to owners, *Alan* and *Ann Potts*, transferring ***Sizing John*** from *Henry De Bromhead*'s yard the previous summer. It is a major loss to National Hunt racing that both *Alan* and *Ann Potts* sadly passed away in 2017. *Alan Potts*, who was 80, suffered a heart attack in November, just a few months after his wife passed away after a long illness, at the age of 69.

A month after his victory in Cheltenham's blue riband event, ***Sizing John*** beat *Djakadam* by a short head in the *Coral Punchestown Gold Cup*. Over seven months later at the shorter distance of 2m4f, he beat the same horse at *Punchestown* yet again, but this time with far more authority, winning by seven lengths in the *John Durkan Memorial Punchestown Chase*. Following this impressive performance, ***Sizing John*** was put to the head of the betting to regain his crown in the 2018 *Timico Cheltenham Gold Cup Chase*. However, a few weeks later, after finishing a well-beaten seventh in the *Leopardstown Christmas Chase*, he was replaced as favourite for the race by *Kempton*'s *32Red*

King George VI Chase winner, *Might Bite*. It is still unclear as to why ***Sizing John*** ran no sort of race at *Leopardstown* and the results of any blood tests, at the time of writing, have yet to be published. What is known is that following an immediate post-race examination, veterinary staff at the track, found ***Sizing John*** to be clinically abnormal. It is hoped that information comes to light that provides an explanation as to why ***Sizing John*** flopped at *Leopardstown*, and why on his 13th start over fences, he finished outside of the front three for the first time in his career. I always believe that the *Cheltenham Gold Cup* is all the better if the defending champion turns up to defend his crown, so I will keep my fingers crossed that ***Sizing John*** takes his place in the line-up, and doesn't become the third *Gold Cup* winner in a row who misses Cheltenham's showpiece event twelve months later.

There were eight **Midnight Legend** festival runners last year, and alongside ***Sizing John***'s *Gold Cup* win, the offspring also managed to reward supporters with two place dividends in Thursday's final two races. I have already referenced ***Potters Legend*** 4th place in the *Fulke Walwyn Kim Muir Challenge Cup Amateur Riders' Handicap Chase*, and 40 minutes earlier, ***Dusky Legend*** (20/1) secured a place in the *Trull House Stud Mares' Novices' Hurdle* for the second year in a row, having finished runner-up in the 2016 running at the more rewarding odds of 50/1.

Come the festival this March, once again, there are likely to be quite a few entries sired by **Midnight Legend**, some towards the front of the betting and perhaps a larger number at much bigger odds of 25/1 or greater. In all likelihood, the progeny's runners will be spread out across a variety of distances, tackling both fences and hurdles. Don't be too concerned about the obstacles being jumped, the distance of the race or the odds on offer. Whatever the race and whatever the odds, backing **Midnight Legend**'s offspring at Cheltenham Festivals has historically been rewarding. Just make sure that your bets are each way.

Milan (GB)

Quote from the 2017 Cheltenham Festival Stallion Guide - "Over the past three festivals, **Milan** bred runners have recorded a win or place from close to one in every three runs."

Milan (20-y-o)							
Race Format	*Miles*	*Won*	*Placed*	*Unplaced*	*Total*	*Win %*	*Place %*
Hurdles	About 2m	1	3	2	6	17%	67%
	About 2m 4f	0	0	8	8	0%	0%
	About 3m	2	2	10	14	14%	29%
Chases	About 2m	0	1	3	4	0%	25%
	About 2m 4f	0	4	3	7	0%	57%
	About 3m	0	3	12	15	0%	20%
	About 4m	2	2	4	8	25%	50%
Bumper	About 2m	0	0	7	7	0%	0%
Total	**2008-2017**	**5**	**15**	**49**	**69**	**7%**	**29%**

As each year passes, **Milan**'s progeny are becoming increasingly consistent in following the trends and statistics of previous festivals. In the past couple of Guides, I have highlighted that in recent seasons, **Milan** bred runners are averaging a win or place from close to one in every three festival runs, and at last year's meeting, it was déjà vu once again, as of the 13 of the offspring that took part at Cheltenham, four of them were placed. At the 2016 Cheltenham Festival, 3 of the 9 **Milan** sired entries registered a win or place. In 2015, it was 4 from 16, 5 from 12 in 2014 and 2 out of 7, in 2013.

It was in 2010 when we saw the first of **Milan**'s stock appear at a festival when ***Shadow Dancer*** finished down the field in the *Coral Cup*. Three years later and the **Milan** sired ***Prince of Pirates*** was lining up in the 2013 *Fulke Walwyn Kim Muir Challenge Cup Handicap Chase*. He was the nineteenth of **Milan**'s offspring to attempt to win a Cheltenham Festival event, but he too failed, finishing 11th at odds of 14/1. The next race was the start of a turnaround in performances for the progeny, when in the last race of that day, the *Glenfarclas Handicap Chase*, run over the cross country course, the **Milan** bred, ***Big Shu***, was victorious at odds of 14/1. Following a 3rd place finish in the 2014 renewal of the race, ***Big Shu***'s Ireland based trainer, *Peter Maher*, was no doubt thinking about having another tilt at this unique festival prize, when to help in the preparations, he entered ***Big Shu*** to tackle the Cheltenham cross country course for a third time on December 12th 2014. Sadly, it was to be ***Big Shu***'s last race when having been pulled up during the race, he died from a suspected heart attack. Still only nine years old, it was a devastating loss for *Derry* owner, *Hugh Duffy*.

The success of ***Big Shu*** in 2013 has been followed by four more Cheltenham victories for **Milan**'s offspring. The *Jessica Harrington* trained ***Jezki***, at 9/1, won the 2014 *Stan James Champion Hurdle Challenge Trophy*, and the following season, ***Martello Tower*** (14/1) was the third of **Milan** bred festival winners, when claiming victory for another lady trainer, *Margaret Mullins*, in the *Albert Bartlett Novices' Hurdle*. Two more wins for **Milan**'s offspring were registered at the 2016 Cheltenham Festival, one of which was also at the rewarding odds of 14/1, as jockey *Davy Russell*, kept ***Mall Dini*** going all the way to the line, to win the *Pertemps Network Final*. The second festival success of this year came in the 2016 renewal of the race in which ***Big Shu*** was successful, the *Glenfarclas Chase*, which was "won" by the 15/8 favourite, ***Josies Orders***, some five months after the race took place! First past the post was *Any Currency*, but on the 25th August 2016, the British

Horseracing Authority (BHA) announced that *Any Currency* had been disqualified from first place following a positive post-race test for the pain killer, triamcinolone acetonide.

The one negative for **Milan** supporters at the 2017 Cheltenham Festival was the absence of a winner, following four successive years of at least one festival victory. Nevertheless, anyone who had blindly backed all thirteen of **Milan**'s offspring last season to a £1.00 each-way stake would have still made a £5.85 return. In point of fact, backing **Milan**'s progeny blind at every one of the past five festivals would have resulted in a profit. For the record, to a £1.00 each-way stake, the returns have been as follows; 2013 - £6.80; 2014 - £12.05; 2015 - £1.93; 2016 - £8.75; 2017 - £5.85; making a grand profit total of £35.38 over the five year period, courtesy of 5 wins and 13 place dividends out of a total of 56 festival appearances.

Even though a winner did not materialise for **Milan** bred runners last year, the prices returned for the placed horses ensured that it would be another profitable festival for the sire's supporters. **Milan**'s offspring got off to a flyer at the 2017 Cheltenham Festival, registering two place dividends within the first three races of the festival. In the festival's second event, the *Racing Post Arkle Challenge Trophy Novices' Chase*, there was no great depth to the race as the *Nicky Henderson* trained, *Altior* (1/4 favourite), had almost certainly scared off a number of other potential entries. Nevertheless, trainer *Henry De Bromhead* must have been very pleased with the performance of ***Ordinary World***, and no doubt too jockey *Davy Russell*, who rode the **Milan** bred gelding more prominently than anticipated, a strategy that helped ***Ordinary World*** to finish third at the rewarding odds of 25/1. In the next race, the *Ultima Handicap Chase* over 3m1f, **Milan** was represented by the well supported 5/1 favourite, ***Singlefarmpayment***, trained by *Tom George*. The horse travelled really well throughout the race, but in the final 100 yards as they approached the winning line, the 7 year old was out battled by the year older and gutsy *Un Temps Pour Tout* who triumphed by a short head, thereby repeating his victory in this race 12 months previously.

The other two place dividends from the progeny were delivered on the last day of the festival. Two **Milan** bred runners lined up at the start of the *Albert Bartlett Novices' Hurdle*, attempting to make it the 3rd year in a row for the offspring to register a victory in a three mile hurdle event, following the success of ***Martello Tower*** in the 2015 running of this race and ***Mall Dini***'s win in the 2016 *Pertemps Network Final*. As it turned out, the *Henry De Bromhead* trained ***Monalee***, couldn't cope with *Penhill* who ran on strongly to win comfortably by 3½ lengths, leaving ***Monalee*** to come home in second at odds of 8/1. The other **Milan** bred runner in the race was the 33/1 outsider, ***Tommy Rapper***, who finished eighth. Two races later and we were just two necks away from a shock 100/1 winner in the shape of ***Barel Of Laughs*** who belied his odds when finishing 3rd in the *St. James's Place Foxhunter Challenge Cup Open Hunters' Chase*. Although outpaced approaching two from home, this 11 year old son of **Milan** rallied up the run-in, just failing to get the better of the *Paul Nicholls* trained duo of *Pacha Du Polder* who won by a neck ahead of *Wonderful Charm*, who in turn finished a neck up on ***Barel Of Laughs***.

In my closing paragraph in last year's Guide, I highlighted that the statistics table of **Milan**'s progeny may suggest that one should only support the offspring in the four categories of 2m hurdles, 3m hurdles, 2½m chases and 4m chases. I was at pains to point out, however, that there was enough evidence to suggest that **Milan** bred runners can and will perform equally as well within the other race categories and so advised punters to support the stock across the board. The 2017 results went some way to justify my view, as **Milan** sired runners secured a place position for the first time within the 2m chase category, and runner-up and third place finishes in the 3m chase division, where previously the progeny had managed just a 4th place dividend from 11 attempts at the distance.

As we approach the 2018 Cheltenham Festival, would I advise punters to blindly back at level stakes all of **Milan**'s offspring that take part? Why not? It is a strategy that has produced a profit at every meeting for the past five years.

Montjeu (IRE)

Quote from the 2017 Cheltenham Festival Stallion Guide - "When it comes to the Cheltenham Festival, my advice to punters is to avoid **Montjeu** sired runners and that includes ***Ivanovich Gorbatov***, should the horse be entered at the 2017 festival. Since the bay gelding's success in the 2016 *JCB Triumph Hurdle*, at the time of writing, ***Ivanovich Gorbatov*** has raced over hurdles on six further occasions and hasn't won any of them."

Montjeu (Died as a 16-y-o in 2012)							
Race Format	*Miles*	*Won*	*Placed*	*Unplaced*	*Total*	*Win %*	*Place %*
Hurdles	About 2m	3	4	26	33	9%	21%
	About 2m 4f	0	0	4	4	0%	0%
	About 3m	0	0	2	2	0%	0%
Chases	About 2m	0	0	1	1	0%	0%
	About 2m 4f	1	0	3	4	25%	25%
	About 3m	0	0	2	2	0%	0%
	About 4m	0	0	0	0	-	-
Bumper	About 2m	0	0	0	0	-	-
Total	**2008-2017**	**4**	**4**	**38**	**46**	**9%**	**17%**

In the 2016 Cheltenham Festival Stallion Guide, I made the bold prediction that ***Hurricane Fly*** would be the last **Montjeu** bred Cheltenham Festival winner, only for ***Ivanovich Gorbatov*** to make me eat my words when romping home in the 2016 *JCB Triumph Hurdle*. Based on my quote from the 2107 Guide (see top of the page), as they lined up for last year's *Randox Health County Handicap Hurdle*, I was praying that the same horse wouldn't once again humiliate me and win again!! Before they set off, I was biting my fingernails to the quick as ***Ivanovich Gorbatov*** was strongly backed into 5/1 favouritism having touched 8/1 as the market opened. Trained by *Joseph Patrick O'Brien*, the **Montjeu** sired five year old ran a solid race, challenging briefly for 2nd place on the run-in but unable to quicken or stay on strongly enough to claim a top four place. He wasn't far away though, finishing in 6th position just three lengths off the eventual winner, top weight *Arctic Fire*. For the record, as of 1st January 2018, ***Ivanovich Gorbatov*** has contested eleven races since his 2016 *JCB Triumph Hurdle* success and has been beaten on every occasion.

I was surprised that ***Ivanovich Gorbatov*** was the only one of **Montjeu**'s progeny to appear at the 2017 Cheltenham Festival. Perhaps owners and trainers are beginning to realise that unless you have a ***Hurricane Fly*** on your hands, entering **Montjeu** bred runners at Cheltenham Festivals is, by and large, a complete waste of time, with the obvious irregularities of ***Noble Prince***, who won the 2011 *Jewson Novices' Chase* and the aforementioned ***Ivanovich Gorbatov***. If one takes out the five heroic performances of ***Hurricane Fly***, **Montjeu** sired runners have recorded two victories and two place dividends from a total of 45 festival races. Moreover, within those 45 events, the progeny have failed to finish in the first eight positions on 29 occasions.

The maverick amongst **Montjeu**'s family was the brilliant ***Hurricane Fly*** who burst onto the festival scene when beating *Peddlers Cross* by just over a length in the 2011 *Stan James Champion Hurdle Challenge Trophy*. Although 4/6 odds-on favourite to retain his *Champion Hurdle* crown a year later, he finished in third place, beaten by *Rock On Ruby*. Twelve months on and ***Hurricane Fly*** would gain revenge on the 2012 winner, beating the *Harry Fry* trained runner by 2½ lengths to lift the *Champion*

Hurdle prize for the second time. In 2014, and now ten years old, he again started as the favourite for the race, but on this occasion, he just missed out on the places, finishing in fourth. His last run in the *Champion Hurdle* was in 2015, when he lined up at odds of 8/1 due no doubt to the fact that he was now 11 years old. Despite his age, the *Champion Hurdle* hero ran brilliantly to finish in third place. It was his fifth consecutive run in the race. When he was retired five months later, having amassed £1,861,015 in prize money, his trainer *Willie Mullins* justifiably stated that he was "the horse of a generation".

Since being gelded in December 2008 to his last appearance at Cheltenham in March 2015, ***Hurricane Fly*** raced exclusively in hurdle events of around two miles, with just one exception in December 2010, when over a distance of 2m4f, he won the *Bar One Racing Hatton's Grace Hurdle* at *Fairyhouse*. Over jumps, the vast majority of **Montjeu** bred runners are like ***Hurricane Fly***, in that the race category where most of the offspring appear is in two mile hurdle races; indeed, specifically at Cheltenham Festivals, 37 of the progeny's 50 appearances have taken place in 2m hurdle contests. All of which, in my analysis, means that the chances of seeing another festival winner sired by **Montjeu** is becoming increasingly remote. In National Hunt racing, one is most likely to see younger horses, aged between say 4 and 6 years old, racing in bumpers or shorter distance hurdle events, with a number of the races being for novices only. As these racehorses get older, they tend to go up in distance and many of them will leave the hurdles behind and be campaigned over fences. **Montjeu** died in 2012 which means that the majority of his stock will be aged six or older, with a handful of five year olds. Even if some of the offspring are high enough in the official ratings to get to a Cheltenham Festival, the current age profile combined with the fact that the progeny rarely race in events other than two mile hurdle contests, suggests that there will be very few festival opportunities where **Montjeu** bred entries are likely to be competitive.

Deeper analysis of the performances of **Montjeu**'s offspring in the festival's two mile contests is quite revealing. Sixteen runs from the progeny have taken place in the two 2m hurdle events that are restricted to four year olds, these being the *Triumph Hurdle* and the *Fred Winter Juvenile Handicap Hurdle*. As advised earlier, ***Ivanovich Gorbatov*** won the 2016 *JCB Triumph Hurdle* and eight years earlier, in the 2008 running of this event, ***Won In The Dark*** finished third. Going back to 2009, in the *Fred Winter Juvenile Novices' Handicap Hurdle*, ***Alexander Severus*** was the warm 5/2 favourite when securing a place dividend by finishing 4th. The three wins and four places that are shown in the 2m hurdle category in the above statistics table represent the three performances highlighted above from **Montjeu** bred four year olds plus ***Hurricane Fly***'s two wins and two places in the *Champion Hurdle*. Take out ***Hurricane Fly*** and in the 16 festival races within the 2m hurdle category for runners aged five or older, **Montjeu**'s representatives have so far failed to register a top four placing. Outside of the festival's 2m hurdle competitions, **Montjeu** has been represented in just 13 races, of which just seven have been over fences. ***Noble Prince***'s victory in the 2011 *Jewson Novices' Chase* was rather untypical, as on the other six occasions, the offspring have finished well behind. And in the six middle and long distance hurdle events in which the stock have competed, performances have been largely uninspiring.

Taking all of the above into account as we approach the 2018 Cheltenham Festival, **Montjeu**'s progeny are too old to run in the four year old events where they have previously had some success, and ***Hurricane Fly*** has long since retired, so it is difficult to see where a winner or even a place position will come from. And looking through the current crop of horses bred by **Montjeu** together with their official ratings, I'm not sure any of them are classy enough to win or be placed in any of the festival races for which they will be eligible. That said, there is potentially one exception, which is the *John P McManus* owned five year old, ***Rhinestone***. At the time of writing, ***Rhinestone*** has an entry in Cheltenham's *Weatherbys Champion Bumper*. If he were to run, it would almost certainly be the one and only time that **Montjeu** will have appeared in Cheltenham's legendary *National Hunt*

Flat Race. Trained by *Joseph Patrick O'Brien*, **Rhinestone** has only appeared on a racecourse twice, the second appearance of which was a 19 length win in the *Ryan Tarmacadam INH Flat Race* at *Thurles* on 17th December 2017. With just two runs under his belt, it is still far too early to make any judgement as to how much ability ***Rhinestone*** possesses, but should he take his chance in the *Bumper* and perform well, you never know, he may be good enough to take his chance in a two mile hurdle event at the 2019 Cheltenham Festival. We will wait and see.

Network (GER)

Network was not featured in the 2017 Cheltenham Festival Stallion Guide.

Network (21-y-o)							
Race Format	*Miles*	*Won*	*Placed*	*Unplaced*	*Total*	*Win %*	*Place %*
Hurdles	About 2m	0	1	1	2	0%	50%
	About 2m 4f	0	1	2	3	0%	33%
	About 3m	0	0	1	1	0%	0%
Chases	About 2m	3	0	2	5	60%	60%
	About 2m 4f	0	1	2	3	0%	33%
	About 3m	0	0	5	5	-	-
	About 4m	0	0	0	0	-	-
Bumper	About 2m	0	0	0	0	-	-
Total	**2008-2017**	**3**	**3**	**13**	**19**	**16%**	**32%**

There have been eight festival appearances from **Network**'s progeny at the past two festivals, which when added to the previous 11 runs, provide early signs of a trend. Preceding 2015, there would only be one **Network** sired horse to talk about, ***Sprinter Sacre***. Even now, one of the best horses to ever be trained by *Nicky Henderson*, still dominates **Network**'s festival statistics.

Sprinter Sacre is now retired from racing but during his racing career, he proved himself to be an outstanding two-mile chaser. He won 18 of his 24 races and amassed over a million pounds in prize money for his owner, *Mrs Caroline Mould*. The last of ***Sprinter Sacre***'s four runs over hurdles was in the first of his five appearances at the Cheltenham Festival when he finished 3rd in the 2011 *Stan James Supreme Novices' Hurdle*. ***Sprinter Sacre*** made his first appearance over fences at *Doncaster* in December 2011 winning the *Atteys Solicitors Novices' Chase* by 24 lengths. It was the first of ten consecutive victories which included two breath-taking performances at the 2012 and 2013 Cheltenham Festivals. In the *Racing Post Arkle Challenge Trophy Chase* on 13th May 2012, ***Sprinter Sacre*** coasted to victory to win by seven lengths from *Cue Card*. The distance could have been a lot further but for jockey *Barry Geraghty* easing him down in the closing stages. The jockey later described the race as the equivalent of a "schooling session". The following season, ***Sprinter Sacre*** started as the 1/4 favourite for the *Sportingbet Queen Mother Champion Chase*, the shortest price at a Cheltenham Festival since *Arkle* won his third *Gold Cup* in 1966. He was never off the bridle and recorded another impressive victory this time by 19 lengths from runner-up *Sizing Europe*.

Nine months later and ***Sprinter Sacre***'s ten race winning run came to an end in dramatic style in the *williamhill.com Desert Orchid Chase* at *Kempton Park*, when the 2/9 favourite was pulled up just after the seventh fence. Post-race tests revealed that he was suffering from an irregular heartbeat and he missed the rest of the season. Over the next eighteen months, ***Sprinter Sacre*** continued to suffer from a series of injury and health problems and it looked as if he would never again experience his previous triumphs. During this period, he was pulled up for the second time in his career in the 2015 *Betway Queen Mother Champion Chase* and retirement of *Nicky Henderson*'s star two-miler was mooted once again.

Many within the Cheltenham crowd were delighted to see ***Sprinter Sacre*** return to the Cheltenham Festival in 2016, and although their hearts may have wanted him to win the *Betway Queen Mother Champion Chase*, many of them were no doubt expecting the likely winner to be the 4/6 favourite,

Un de Sceaux, the highly impressive 2015 winner of the *Arkle*. ***Sprinter Sacre*** lined up as the 5/1 second favourite for the 2016 *Queen Mother Champion Chase* and although he didn't win with the same ease with which he had won the race three years previously, it was an incredible performance by the ten year old to beat the odds-on favourite. ***Sprinter Sacre*** was wearing earplugs during the race but I'm certain they wouldn't have been able to drown out the incredible noise from the grandstands once he had safely cleared the last fence. The reception that the horse received after the race is something I will remember for years to come.

Monty Python used to say "And now for something completely different", and in comparison to ***Sprinter Sacre***, that is how I would describe the four performances from the four **Network** bred runners that appeared at the 2017 Cheltenham festival. To be fair, three of the runners lined up at big prices; ***Bon Papa*** (18/1) was pulled up in the *Neptune Investment Management Novices' Hurdle*; ***Venitien De Mai*** (25/1) fell at the 9th whilst contending the *Fulke Walwyn Kim Muir Challenge Cup Amateur Riders' Handicap Chase*; and ***Catamaran Du Seuil*** (33/1) was 20th and last of those that completed the course in the *Martin Pipe Conditional Jockeys' Handicap Hurdle*. The remaining runner at last year's meeting, ***Acapella Bourgeois***, was much more fancied in the market and lined up in the *RSA Novices' Chase* at a price of 5/1. In the race, the joint 3rd favourite didn't appear to enjoy the quicker ground, and *Acapella Bourgeois* weakened quickly and was tailed to finish in sixth place over 60 lengths away from the winner.

If we discount the exceptional ***Sprinter Sacre*** from the statistics table above, then we are left with 10 of **Network**'s offspring competing in 14 festival races, nine within which the **Network** sired runner competed at odds of 18/1 or greater. And although nine runs is not a huge statistical baseline upon which to make a concrete judgement, if you are one of those punters who likes a bet on big priced outsiders, then my advice is to look elsewhere. In those nine runs where the runner sired by **Network** lined up at odds of 18/1 or bigger, four failed to complete the race and three more finished 12th, 14th and 20th. The best two runs from **Network** sired outsiders happened at the 2016 Cheltenham Festival where ***Allysson Monterg*** (40/1) finished 6th in the *Albert Bartlett Novices' Hurdle* and *Workbench* (33/1) came home in 8th position in the *Johnny Henderson Grand Annual Chase Challenge Cup*.

If we again omit ***Sprinter Sacre*** from the data, it is clear that the performances are much more encouraging from the small sample of **Network** bred festival runners that competed at odds of 16/1 or shorter. In 2016, ***Blazer*** was successful in rewarding each-way backers when he finished 4th at a price of 8/1 in the *Coral Cup*, just a couple of lengths away from the winner, *Diamond King*. Another place dividend for **Network**'s stock was achieved by ***Rubi Light*** five years earlier. Trained by *Robert Alan Hennessy*, ***Rubi Light*** ran at two consecutive Cheltenham Festival Meetings in 2011 and 2012, where on both occasions he took on older horses in the *Ryanair Chase*. Lining up as a six year old, and at least two years younger than his ten competitors in the 2011 renewal, it was quite an achievement to take third place at a price of 16/1, beaten by two of the three 10 year olds in the race. In the 2012 running, a year older and at a price of 13/2, ***Rubi Light*** was once again the youngest in the race, but he was unable to match the previous year's effort and he came home in 5th position.

The other two of **Network**'s offspring to be sent off at odds shorter than 16/1, both raced in the *RSA Chase* with ***Adriana Des Mottes*** just missing out on a place dividend when finishing fourth by just a head, in the 2015 contest. As well as being the only mare in the race, the 14/1 chance was also the youngest at just five years old. She put up a gallant effort on her first attempt at three miles. The sixth place of ***Acapella Bourgeois*** in the 2017 *RSA Novices' Chase* has already been highlighted.

Network's festival statistics table show a 16% win strike rate and a 32% win and place strike rate which is impressive, but let's not forget that the three victories and one of the places have been recorded by the exceptional talent that was ***Sprinter Sacre***. For our analysis, we need to concentrate on the 14 results delivered by the other ten of **Network**'s stock that have raced at the festival. And in that regard, although 14 runs is a small sample on which to pick out any trends, and albeit that the market should be a reasonably accurate guide to performance, with **Network**'s progeny, there does appear to be a very clear division in the festival results of those that have lined up at odds of 18/1 plus and those that have competed at odds of 16/1 or shorter. Specifically, of the five runners that were sent off at odds of 16/1 or shorter, four of the finishing positions were 3rd, 4th, 4th and 5th with two of the representatives rewarding each-way bets with a place dividend.

It is clearly early days and further future runs from **Network**'s stock will help to firm up any initial conclusions, but at this moment in time, I would advise punters that if they are interested in any of **Network**'s representatives at the 2018 Cheltenham Festival, they should concentrate their efforts on those at the front of the betting market at around 16/1 or shorter.

Old Vic (GB)

Quote from the 2017 Cheltenham Festival Stallion Guide - "Finally, I need to highlight the *Fulke Walwyn Kim Muir Challenge Cup Handicap Chase*. This has been a strikingly rewarding race for **Old Vic** supporters over the past five years, where the progeny have a 100% record of securing a win or place dividend."

Old Vic (Died as a 25-y-o in 2011)							
Race Format	Miles	Won	Placed	Unplaced	Total	Win %	Place %
Hurdles	About 2m	0	0	3	3	0%	0%
	About 2m 4f	3	1	10	14	21%	29%
	About 3m	0	2	15	17	0%	12%
Chases	About 2m	0	0	1	1	0%	0%
	About 2m 4f	1	3	10	14	7%	29%
	About 3m	2	4	21	27	7%	22%
	About 4m	0	1	4	5	0%	20%
Bumper	About 2m	0	0	5	5	0%	0%
Total	**2008-2017**	**6**	**11**	**69**	**86**	**7%**	**20%**

On the Thursday at last year's Cheltenham Festival, I was patiently waiting with eager anticipation the last event of the day in which I had picked out the **Old Vic** sired nine year old, ***Pendra***, as my best bet of the day. **Old Vic**'s stock have a fantastic record in this race named *The Fulke Walwyn Kim Muir Challenge Cup Amateur Riders' Handicap Chase*, in which over the past five years, the progeny have a 100% record of finishing in the top four positions. ***Sunnyhillboy*** won the event in 2012, and two years later, ***Spring Heeled*** recorded a second victory for **Old Vic** bred entries, when claiming first place at odds of 12/1. In 2015, ***Grand Vision*** secured a fourth place dividend at odds of 11/1, which was followed in 2016 with two further place positions, when ***Silvergrove*** and ***Knock House***, both at odds of 16/1, finished 3rd and 4th respectively. Backing all five runners in the *Kim Muir* from 2012 onwards would have resulted in a handsome reward of £30.88 to a £1.00 each-way stake, and I was very hopeful that ***Pendra*** would continue the trend and add to the profit figures.

Not only was ***Pendra*** sired by **Old Vic**, but he was also to be assisted by the top class amateur jockey, *Derek O'Connor*, who has won well over 1,000 wins in point-to-points and is a three times winner at previous Cheltenham Festivals. The record of ***Pendra***'s owner, *John P McManus*, in this particular contest, also boosted my confidence. His distinctive green and gold hooped racing colours were victorious in 2012 with the aforementioned ***Sunnyhillboy***, and again in 2016 when *Cause Of Causes* was the victor. Finally, I was not the slightest bit concerned that ***Pendra*** was the top-weight in the race. Indeed, since the *Kim Muir* became a 0-145 handicap in 2012, all five victors had an official rating of 137 or above, with those at or near the top of the weights performing well. ***Sunnyhillboy*** was victorious in 2012 when just 1lb off top weight; *Super Duty* (joint top weight in 2013) finished 2nd by a head; top-weight *Roberto Goldback* finished 3rd in 2014 and ***Knock House*** was just 1lb off top weight when finishing 4th in 2016.

At a starting price of 16/1 and sporting first-time blinkers, ***Pendra*** was always up with the pace, either disputing the lead or tracking the leaders. *Derek O'Connor* made his move two out, driving ***Pendra*** to forge clear, so that at the last, the *Charlie Longsdon* trained top weight was some three lengths up. My excitement started to drain away, as up the famous Cheltenham Hill, my fancy drifted right under pressure and the rest of the field started to close. ***Pendra*** had run a huge race, but in the end had no extra to give, as the 40/1 outsider, *Domesday Book*, rallied well after the last to take the prize by just under a length. So near, yet so far. It was a galling loss.

Due to **Old Vic**'s death in 2011, this stallion's remaining stock are now in their later years and, as a result, those that appear at the 2018 Cheltenham Festival are most likely to appear in the longer distance chase events. The youngest of **Old Vic**'s entries will be eight years old, which means that across 24 of the 28 races at this year's meeting, I expect there to be perhaps a combined total of 2 or 3 declared **Old Vic** sired runners. The vast majority of winners in these 24 contests are 7 year olds or younger, so the chances of **Old Vic**'s offspring recording a success in these races is highly improbable. There are four festival contests, however, like the *Kim Muir*, where older chasers are not only widely represented, but also can win. The four races to focus upon are *The Ultima Handicap Steeple Chase* (3m1f); *The Glenfarclas Cross Country Steeple Chase* (3m6f); *The Fulke Walwyn Kim Muir Challenge Cup Handicap Steeple Chase* (3m2f); and *The St. James's Place Foxhunter Steeple Chase Challenge Cup* (3m2½f). Taking all four events together over the past decade, 32 of the 40 winners have been aged eight or older.

Unfortunately for the stallion's supporters, the performances of **Old Vic** bred runners in two of these four events leave a lot to be desired. In the *Foxhunters*, the first four appearances from the offspring resulted in the runner being pulled up. At least, at last year's festival, the two **Old Vic** sired entries, ***Minella For Value*** (100/1) and ***Grand Vision*** (50/1), managed to complete the course. In the *Ultima Handicap Steeple Chase*, our old friend ***Pendra*** had produced the best performance when finishing in 5th place in the 2015 contest. On the other eight occasions where **Old Vic** has been listed as the sire, there has only been one other top ten finish, courtesy of ***Comply or Die***'s 7th placing in 2009. It is too early to make any conclusions with regard to *The Glenfarclas Cross Country Steeple Chase*, as **Old Vic**'s progeny have only been represented in this event on two occasions. All of the above brings us back to the *Kim Muir* as the best race on which to focus our attention, where in chronological order, **Old Vic** bred runners have recorded finishing positions of 6th, 1st, 1st, 4th, 3rd, 4th, 2nd and 12th. If one had backed all eight runners blind to a £1.00 each-way stake, the resultant profit would have been a very satisfying £29.88.

Readers of previous Cheltenham Festival Stallion Guides will be well aware that within the commentary about **Old Vic**, I have highlighted how well the progeny perform in *Aintree*'s *Grand National*. In short, there is a clear correlation showing that horses that have contested a 3m race at a Cheltenham Festival, very often perform well in *Grand Nationals*. In the 2016 running of the *Crabbie's Grand National Chase*, for example, who would have considered that the thirteen year old ***Vic's Canvas***, who set off as the 100/1 outsider of the entire field, would finish a gallant 3rd in the race, even more remarkable, considering that having blundered badly at *Becher's Brook*, first time round, jockey *Richard Dunne* was halfway over the side and hanging off the horse's neck but somehow managed to stay aboard. ***Vic's Canvas*** had just about contested a three mile race at Cheltenham previously – he fell at the very first hurdle in the 2014 *Pertemps Network Final*! In finishing third, ***Vic's Canvas*** is one of seven **Old Vic** sired horses to finish in the first four in the last ten *Grand Nationals*. And all seven of them had previously contested a three mile event at a Cheltenham Festival. This equates to 17½% of the top four places being reserved for **Old Vic**'s progeny, which, for a race often described (mistakenly in my view) as a lottery, is some achievement. For the record, the seven Old Vic sired top four *Grand National* finishers are as follows:

2008 – 1st ***Comply or Die*** (previously runner-up in the 2005 *Royal & SunAlliance Chase)*
2009 – 2nd ***Comply or Die*** (previously 7th in the 2009 *William Hill Trophy Handicap Chase*)
2010 – 1st ***Don't Push It*** (previously pulled up in the 2010 *Pertemps Final*)
2010 – 2nd ***Black Apalachi*** (previously 6th in the 2006 *Fulke Walwyn Kim Muir Handicap Chase)*
2011 – 3rd ***Don't Push It*** (previously 10th in the 2011 *Pertemps Final*)
2012 – 2nd ***Sunnyhillboy*** (previously 1st in the 2012 *Fulke Walwyn Kim Muir Handicap Chase)*

2016 – 3rd ***Vic's Canvas*** (previously fell in the 2014 *Pertemps Final*)

Old Vic was unrepresented in last season's *Randox Health Grand National Handicap Chase*. ***Knock House*** was a reserve, failing to make the list of 40 runners due to not quite being high enough in the handicap ratings, and ***Pendra*** was withdrawn from the contest 48 hours before race day. Come the marathon event in April 2018, I will still be very interested in any declared runners where **Old Vic** is listed as the sire. It is still early days, but at the time of writing, potential names to look out for are ***Audacious Plan***, ***Folsom Blue***, ***Knock House***, ***Pendra*** and ***Southfield Vic***.

As regards to the 2018 Cheltenham Festival, I consider it futile to try and find an **Old Vic** festival winner from anywhere except within the four races highlighted earlier, with Thursday's *Fulke Walwyn Kim Muir Challenge Cup Handicap Steeple Chase* being the race in which bets on **Old Vic**'s offspring are most likely to deliver rewards. For the more devoted fans of this stallion, the other three festival races where an **Old Vic** sired winner may potentially emerge is from the *Ultima Handicap Steeple Chase*, The *Glenfarclas Cross Country Steeple Chase* and The *St. James's Place Foxhunter Steeple Chase Challenge Cup*.

Oscar (IRE)

Quote from the 2017 Cheltenham Festival Stallion Guide - "I cannot provide a logical explanation, but when it comes to the Cheltenham Festival, **Oscar**'s offspring have a far less impressive record in the handicap events."

Oscar (24-y-o)							
Race Format	*Miles*	*Won*	*Placed*	*Unplaced*	*Total*	*Win %*	*Place %*
Hurdles	About 2m	1	5	9	15	7%	40%
	About 2m 4f	2	3	15	20	10%	25%
	About 3m	1	4	23	28	4%	18%
Chases	About 2m	1	4	6	11	9%	45%
	About 2m 4f	0	0	12	12	0%	0%
	About 3m	3	4	23	30	10%	23%
	About 4m	2	0	5	7	29%	29%
Bumper	About 2m	0	0	7	7	0%	0%
Total	**2008-2017**	**10**	**20**	**100**	**130**	**8%**	**23%**

Is the Cheltenham Festival Stallion Guide putting a jinx on **Oscar**? Ever since I started writing the Guide in 2015, **Oscar**'s stock have yet to record a festival winner. And yet, in the preceding nine years, **Oscar**'s offspring were victorious on 12 occasions, only failing to record a festival winner at the 2011 meeting. Backing blind, £1.00 each way, on all runners sired by **Oscar** between 2006 and 2014 would have delivered a profit at five of those festival meetings, with an overall profit over the nine years of £20.25. The losses incurred, had one backed every **Oscar** bred runner at the past three Cheltenham Festivals, would have been £39.05 to a £1.00 each-way stake.

Over the past three seasons, it could be argued that the poor results are a reflection of **Oscar**'s festival representatives being largely unfancied in the market. And indeed, only 12% (4 of 33) of **Oscar** sired festival runners between 2015 and 2017, lined up at single figure odds. This compares with 24% (25 of 106) of **Oscar**'s representatives racing at single figure odds between the 2006 and 2014 festival meetings. Even though the logic makes sense, I'm not convinced. Within this Guide, there are a number of examples where the analysis of a sire's festival record, based upon the performance of that sire's offspring, will conclude that the starting prices of the runners appear to be a very significant factor in deciding whether or not a sire's progeny will run well. This is not the case with **Oscar**. Of the twelve festival victories recorded by **Oscar**'s progeny, seven of them entered the Winners Enclosure at double figure odds, ranging from 10/1 to 20/1. It should also be noted that between 2006 and 2009, with only 4 of the 32 representatives (12½%) racing at under 10/1, **Oscar**'s offspring still managed to achieve a victory at all four festival meetings. This coming March, for **Oscar** supporters, let's hope for a change in fortune.

If an **Oscar** bred is to bag a winner at the 2018 Cheltenham Festival, the trends suggest that the victory will come in one of the festival's non-handicap races. In the past decade, all 46 of **Oscar**'s representatives who lined up in the festival's handicap races have failed to win, and only six runners achieved a place dividend, which is a strike rate of 13%. The offspring's performances in the festival's non-handicaps are far superior, with 10 victories and 14 places from 84 attempts, resulting in a 12% win strike rate and a 29% win/place strike rate. Placing a £1.00 each-way bet on all 130 festival appearances of **Oscar**'s stock in the past decade would have produced a profit of £28.85 in the non-handicap contests and a loss of £45.25 in the festival's handicap races. ***Oscar Park*** is the only one of **Oscar**'s progeny to be successful in a festival handicap, winning at odds of 14/1 and over a decade ago, in the 2007 *Pertemps Final.*

Considering the record of the offspring in the festival's handicaps, it was something of a shock that an **Oscar** sired runner managed to take 3rd place, at the rewarding odds of 50/1, in last year's Grade 3 *Randox Health County Handicap Hurdle*. ***Ozzie The Oscar***, trained by *Philip Hobbs* and ridden by *Tom O'Brien*, almost won the race, leading 100 yards from home before being narrowly beaten by *Arctic Fire*, who finished a neck in front of runner-up, *L'Ami Serge*. Achieving a placing in a festival handicap does not happen that often for **Oscar**'s progeny, but even more infrequent is a placed effort in a handicap at a distance below three miles. The results for **Oscar** bred runners in 2 and 2½ mile handicaps at Cheltenham Festivals have been absolutely dire. In 21 appearances, nineteen runners have either failed to complete the course or have finished 10th or worse. The two exceptions being ***Askthemaster***, who was runner-up in the 2011 running of the *Johnny Henderson Grand Annual Chase Challenge Cup*, and the aforementioned ***Ozzie The Oscar*** last season. Both runners achieved their place dividends at odds of 50/1.

The results for **Oscar**'s stock are better in three mile festival handicaps, albeit still not as fruitful as the performances in the longer distance non-handicap events. In the Cheltenham Festival's only three mile handicap hurdle contest, the *Pertemps Final*, fourteen **Oscar** sired runners have competed of which six have managed to trouble the judge, by finishing in the top six positions. As well as the victory by ***Oscar Park*** in the 2007 renewal, two more of the progeny filled 2nd and 3rd places in the 2013 running, when ***Captain Sunshine*** (2nd) and ***Jetson*** (3rd) were comfortably beaten by *Holywell*. The only other 3m festival handicap race of interest, come March, is the 3m1f *Ultima Handicap Steeple Chase*, which coincidentally is another race in which *Holywell* has been successful, finishing runner-up in 2016 and winning the 2014 renewal, when it was named the *Baylis & Harding Affordable Luxury Handicap Chase*. In between these two races, in the 2015 contest, the County Meath based trainer, *Tony Martin*, who has enjoyed a number of Cheltenham Festival successes, saw his ***Gallant Oscar*** (9/1) finish 3rd and some five lengths behind clear winner, *The Druids Nephew*. Five years earlier, in 2010, when the race was titled the *William Hill Trophy Handicap Chase*, another Irish trained **Oscar** sired runner, ***Offshore Account***, earned a place dividend when *David Casey* rode the *Charlie Swan* trained runner into 4th position at odds of 33/1.

Turning to the non-handicap festival contests, Oscar's progeny have a very impressive set of statistics in the 2 and 2½ mile hurdle contests. In a total of 22 races, **Oscar** bred runners have hit a top six spot on no less than sixteen occasions, recording three victories and nine others who finished 2nd or 3rd. It is a bizarre and striking set of performances compared to the handicap events in the 2 and 2½ mile categories where in all 13 appearances, other than ***Ozzie The Oscar***'s 3rd place finish in last year's *County Handicap Hurdle*, every single runner either failed to complete the course or recorded a position of 10th or worse! Punters may be interested to know that had one backed all 22 of **Oscar**'s offspring in non-handicap 2m and 2½ mile festival hurdle events, it would have resulted in a profitable return of £28.20 to a £1.00 each-way stake.

Come the 2018 Cheltenham Festival, punters will need to be far more selective in *The Sun Bets Stayers' Hurdle* and *The Albert Bartlett Novices' Hurdle*, these being the festival's two non-handicap long distance hurdle contests. **Oscar** has been represented with 20 runners in these two races over the years, with half of the runners managing a top six finish. For **Oscar** supporters, backing all 20 runners at £1.00 each way would have resulted in the two very short priced victories and two 3rd places, returning a loss of £25.35.

In analysing the performances of **Oscar**'s offspring in non-handicaps over fences, although it is perfectly possible to point to profits and losses in the four distance categories or highlight specific races in which **Oscar**'s stock have performed well, I believe the conclusions drawn may be misleading. For example, if we take the two mile non-handicap chases, it shows 1 victory and 3 places from 11 runs and a profit of £3.50 to a £1.00 each-way stake. On closer examination, the impressive results are primarily down to the *Colm Murphy* trained, ***Big Zeb***, who ran in the *Queen Mother Champion Chase* between 2009 and 2012 and having won the event in 2010, followed up with two placed efforts in the next two renewals.

Oscar, who was retired from his stallion duties in 2015, has produced not only Big Zeb, but also a number of other notable performers over fences including ***Lord Windermere***, ***God's Own***, ***O'Faolains Boy*** and ***Oscar Delta***. If, for the moment, we ignore four mile chases, and just focus on all non-handicap festival chases in the three categories of three miles or shorter, there have been 37 runs from **Oscar** sired horses, which has resulted in four victories and five place positions, which means that supporters typically will pick up at least a place for one in every four bets on **Oscar**'s offspring in a non-handicap festival chase event, excluding the 4m *National Hunt Chase*. However, the influence of just three of **Oscar**'s progeny is very significant. As mentioned earlier, ***Big Zeb*** is responsible for one win and two places; ***Lord Windermere*** is responsible for two victories, and at rewarding odds of 8/1 and 20/1; and ***Oscar Delta***, who had it not been for jinking left and unseating jockey *Jane Mangan* yards from the finishing line in 2013, would have added a *Foxhunters* victory to the two big price 3rd place finishes secured in the previous two renewals. Hence, within the 37 races featured within this analysis, these three **Oscar** bred horses are responsible for all bar two of the nine win and place positions advised earlier.

Based on the thinking above, I believe that in non-handicap festival chases in all bar the 4m category, **Oscar** supporters are best advised to ascertain who amongst **Oscar**'s progeny are going to be the next ***Big Zeb***, ***Lord Windermere*** or ***Oscar Delta***. At the time of writing, it would appear that two of the potential candidates are ***River Wylde*** and ***Finian's Oscar*** and if I had to make a decision on which of the two is the more likely to win a Cheltenham Festival race, I would plump for the latter. ***Finian's Oscar*** was purchased for £250,000 a few months before last year's festival by the late *Alan* and *Ann Potts*, both of whom sadly passed away in 2017.

A winner of his first three hurdle appearances, including the Grade 1 *32Red Tolworth Novices' Hurdle* at Sandown, ***Finian's Oscar*** was made favourite for the *Neptune Investment Management Novices' Hurdle*, before a minor setback just a week before the festival meeting, ruled him out. A few weeks later, and the *Colin Tizzard* trained gelding was back and winning yet again in the *Betway Mersey Novices Hurdle (Grade 1)* at *Aintree*. As for ***River Wylde***, having also won his first three novice hurdles, *Nicky Henderson* entered him in the festival's opener, the *Sky Bet Supreme Novices' Hurdle*. Ridden by *Nico de Boinville*, ***River Wylde*** ran well to secure 3rd place, albeit some 10 lengths behind surprise winner, *Labaik*, who had a history of refusing to start his races. At the time of writing, both ***Finian's Oscar*** and ***River Wylde*** hold entries in the 2m *Racing Post Arkle Challenge Trophy Novices' Chase* and the *JLT Novices' Chase*, run over a distance of 2m4f. ***Finian's Oscar*** also has an entry in the *RSA Novices' Chase* over 3m½f. If ***River Wylde*** is to have a chance in either of the his two festival entries, he will need to do a lot better than his disappointing run in the *November Novices Chase* at *Cheltenham*, which was run on soft, tacky ground on 19th November. ***River Wylde*** finished 2nd of three runners in the race, some 18 lengths behind the winner, *North Hill Harvey*. Two days before the *November Novices' Chase*, ***Finian's Oscar*** also had an outing at *Cheltenham*, with an impressive victory in *The Steel Plate and Sections Novices' Chase*. Punters take note. ***Finian's Oscar*** looks the part to me.

To complete the picture for performances over fences, I would certainly not be put off in backing **Oscar**'s progeny in the *National Hunt Chase* which is for amateur riders and run over a distance of four miles. **Oscar** bred runners have won twice in their five runs to date, with victories secured by ***Tricky Trickster*** at 11/1 in 2009, and ***Teaforthree***, the *Rebecca Curtis* trained 5/1 favourite, in 2012.

Looking forward to the 2018 Cheltenham Festival, if we start with races of around three miles and more, for the most part, my view is that **Oscar** sired winners will be difficult to find, especially in the four races where **Oscar**'s offspring occasionally pop up with a winner or place, these events being the 3rd race of the opening day, the *Ultima Handicap Steeple Chase* and the three long distance hurdle races. For non-handicap festival chases below four miles, my view is that we need to place our bets on the next ***Big Zeb*** or ***Lord Windermere*** and I have highlighted that ***Finian's Oscar*** may fit the bill. And when it comes to Tuesday's *JT McNamara National Hunt Steeple Chase Challenge Cup*, a wager on an **Oscar** sired runner could be worthwhile as historically, **Oscar**'s representatives have a very fair record.

Alternatively, if you want to make things simpler and cut to the chase, the first and best place to start with **Oscar**'s offspring is to list out all the festival's 2m and 2½m hurdle races and then to sort those races into handicap races and non-handicap races. If you come across any **Oscar** sired entries in the 2m and 2½m handicap contests, then strike a line through them, as the trends suggest that they will finish well down the field. If, on the other hand, you find **Oscar**'s progeny listed amongst the runners in the non-handicap 2m and 2½m races, then you should seriously consider placing an each way bet. On 22 previous runs in these events, **Oscar**'s representatives have finished in the top three positions on 12 occasions.

Poliglote (GB)

Quote from the 2017 Cheltenham Festival Stallion Guide - "Come the 2017 Cheltenham Festival, it is a given that **Poliglote**'s progeny should be treated with the utmost respect."

Poliglote (26-y-o)							
Race Format	*Miles*	**Won**	**Placed**	**Unplaced**	**Total**	**Win %**	**Place %**
Hurdles	About 2m	1	3	4	8	13%	50%
	About 2m 4f	2	1	4	7	29%	43%
	About 3m	0	0	2	2	0%	0%
Chases	About 2m	0	0	2	2	0%	0%
	About 2m 4f	0	1	4	5	0%	20%
	About 3m	1	2	2	5	20%	60%
	About 4m	0	0	1	1	0%	0%
Bumper	About 2m	0	0	0	0	-	-
Total	**2008-2017**	**4**	**7**	**19**	**30**	**13%**	**37%**

All four **Poliglote** bred runners that appeared at the 2017 Cheltenham Festival secured a top four finishing position; so the recommendation within last year's Stallion Guide to treat **Poliglote**'s progeny with the utmost respect turned out to be sound advice.

We had to wait until Thursday's opening contest before we would see the first of **Poliglote**'s offspring at last year's festival and of the eight runners to face the starter in the *JLT Novices' Chase*, two of them were sired by **Poliglote**. It was an exciting race with a fair pace throughout and as they came around the final turn, there appeared to be four runners in with a chance, including the two **Poliglote** representatives, ***Top Notch*** and ***Politologue***. The latter, trained by *Paul Nicholls*, had to settle for 4th place, the 10/1 shot unable to match the pace of his rivals and running on at the one pace. Finishing in the runner up position was ***Top Notch*** (7/2) who ran on really well up the Cheltenham Hill but was no match for the impressive *Yorkhill*, who surprisingly turned out to be the first winner of the festival for trainer *Willie Mullins*. By the end of the day, the lauded trainer had won another three races, and following two more successes on Friday, he and *Gordon Elliott* ended up with six wins apiece.

Later in the afternoon in the penultimate race, the 11/8 favourite for the second ever running of the *Trull House Stud Mares' Novices' Hurdle*, was the **Poliglote** sired ***Let's Dance***. Trained by *Willie Mullins* and given a great ride by *Ruby Walsh*, she quickened away on the run-in and won easily. It was the second time ***Let's Dance*** had raced at the festival, having finished 4th in the 2016 *JCB Triumph Hurdle*. Interestingly, the other event dedicated for mares at the festival, the *OLBG Mares' Hurdle* which takes place on the Tuesday, was won by *Apple's Jade*, who was also beaten in the 2016 *Triumph*, when finishing runner-up. As a pointer perhaps to the 2018 Cheltenham Festival, the horse that claimed 3rd place, finishing between the two mares, was *Footpad*, who at the time of writing is the favourite for the *Racing Post Arkle Challenge Trophy Novices' Chase*.

The fourth of **Poliglote**'s representatives at the 2017 Cheltenham Festival was ***Wonderful Charm*** who finished runner-up, by a neck, in the *St James's Place Foxhunter Challenge Cup Open Hunters' Chase*. It was a very satisfying race for trainer *Paul Nicholls* who saddled both ***Wonderful Charm*** (7/2) and the winner, *Pacha Du Polder* (16/1), who finished 5th in the previous year's renewal of the race, when ridden by *Victoria Pendleton*.

If we look at the festival data for **Poliglote**'s progeny, 17 of the offspring have made a total of 32 festival appearances. Two of those appearances aren't included in the table as they occurred over a decade ago, but the second of the runs is worth noting as it resulted in a victory for the *Jonjo O'Neill* trained, ***Butler's Cabin*** (33/1), who landed the 2007 *National Hunt Chase Challenge Cup*. The victory was a sign of things to come, as **Poliglote** sired runners have continued to perform consistently well at Cheltenham Festivals ever since. From 32 festival runs, five victories and seven places from the offspring translate into impressive strike rates of a 16% chance of winning a race and a 22% chance of finishing 2nd or 3rd. Another 7 of the 32 runs from the progeny resulted in finishing positions of 4th, 5th or 6th which means that historically, for every five festival appearances, **Poliglote**'s representatives are hitting a top six finishing position in three of them. In the two mile hurdle category, from 8 runs in total, only two **Poliglote** bred runners have failed to finish in the front 5, and those two were 25/1 and 66/1 outsiders. In the seven 2½m hurdle events contested by the offspring, the runners have secured a top 4 position on four occasions. And over the larger obstacles, if we combine the results of chases within the 2½m and 3m categories, from 11 runs in total, **Poliglote**'s representatives have finished in the first six positions on eight occasions.

The statistics are highly impressive which is why we should be very interested in **Poliglote**'s stock at Cheltenham Festivals, as no doubt, the offspring will continue to perform. However, there is a spanner in the works, as somewhat surprisingly, making a profitable return from such excellent festival results has not been as easy as one would expect. If we take the results overall, then a £1.00 each way bet on all 32 festival runs from **Poliglote**'s progeny at Cheltenham Festivals, would have resulted in a total profit of £34.95. However, this profit is largely influenced by the three bigger priced winners; ***Butler's Cabin*** at 33/1 in the 2007 *National Hunt Chase Challenge Cup*; ***Spirit River*** at 14/1 in the 2010 *Coral Cup*; and ***Don Poli*** at 14/1 in the 2014 *Martin Pipe Conditional Jockeys' Handicap Hurdle*. Indeed, if we take the eleven festivals that have taken place between 2007 and 2017, it is only in the three years when these big priced wins occurred (2007, 2010 and 2014) that backing **Poliglote**'s representatives blind to level stakes would have resulted in making a profit. In 2008, there were no festival runners sired by **Poliglote**, but in the other seven years, blindly supporting all of the offspring would have resulted in a loss.

I'm convinced that it is largely a quirk of fate that has thrown up a fascinating set of results and starting prices that combined together has resulted in so many loss-making years. One only has to look at the results in detail. Of the 19 **Poliglote** sired runners who lined up at odds of 10/1 or greater, three of them won, as highlighted above. Of the remaining 16, all of them failed to register a place, although five were relatively close, finishing 4th, 5th or 6th. Two of the offspring were sent off as short priced favourites, 11/8 and 13/8, both of which won. All of which leaves us with another eleven runners who had starting prices from a low of 3/1 and a high of 9/1. None of them won, but seven of them finished 2nd or 3rd, six of them between the narrow band of 3/1 and 5/1, prices where each-way wagers typically result in a small loss. If we had a crystal ball which told us that results will continue this way, the most profitable staking plan would be to put large win bets on any **Poliglote** bred favourite with odds of 2/1 or less (100% record so far!); Go to the Tote and put on 'Place Only' bets for any of the progeny who have single figure odds bigger than 2/1 (historically you would win twice in every 3 bets!); and put win only bets on all the other runners (where **Poliglote** bred runners provide a big priced winner once in every six races!).

Although it has been a little cumbersome to work out a profitable staking strategy for this stallion's runners, it should not deflect us away from the compelling reality. When it comes to Cheltenham Festivals, **Poliglote**'s progeny deliver high quality performances, consistently, year after year.

Presenting (GB)

Quote from the 2017 Cheltenham Festival Stallion Guide - "There were 22 horses sired by **Presenting** that ran at last season's Cheltenham Festival and ***Yorkhill*** was the solitary winner, thereby continuing the recent trend of **Presenting**'s progeny of providing one victory per festival."

Presenting (Died as a 25-y-o in 2017)							
Race Format	*Miles*	*Won*	*Placed*	*Unplaced*	*Total*	*Win %*	*Place %*
Hurdles	About 2m	0	3	5	8	0%	38%
	About 2m 4f	2	1	22	25	8%	12%
	About 3m	2	2	15	19	11%	21%
Chases	About 2m	0	0	10	10	0%	0%
	About 2m 4f	3	6	16	25	12%	36%
	About 3m	4	9	37	50	8%	26%
	About 4m	0	2	20	22	0%	9%
Bumper	About 2m	1	1	11	13	8%	15%
Total	**2008-2017**	**12**	**24**	**136**	**172**	**7%**	**21%**

The most prevalent stallion for horses competing at the Cheltenham Festival over the past decade, is **Presenting**, with 104 of his offspring registering 172 runs between them. So, in late August last year, it was with great sadness when I heard that this wonderful jumps stallion, who had finished 3rd in the 1995 *Derby*, had been put down due to the infirmities of old age at the age of 25. **Presenting** has been a legend at the *Glenview Stud* for 20 years, finishing within the top six of leading jumps sires by prize money in Britain and Ireland in every season since 2005-06 and being crowned champion on four occasions. Over his lifetime, his jumps progeny have amassed prize-money earnings in excess of £22 million.

Without doubt, the most famous of **Presenting**'s offspring is ***Denman***, who raced at the Cheltenham Festival for six consecutive seasons (2006–2011) recording two victories and four runner-up spots. The 2006 *Royal & SunAlliance Novices' Hurdle* over 2m5f was ***Denman***'s first festival appearance and his fifth and very last race over the smaller obstacles. The Paul Nicholls trained 11/10 favourite was unbeaten in his previous four hurdle races and so was well fancied to win the race, but ***Denman*** tired up the run-in and was beaten into second spot by the *Noel Meade* trained, *Nicanor*. After the defeat, ***Denman*** was campaigned successfully over fences, and went one better at the following season's festival, when travelling strongly throughout to justify his 6/5 starting price and win the *Royal & SunAlliance Chase* by 10 lengths from *Snowy Morning*. His next four appearances at the festival were all to be in the *Cheltenham Gold Cup*, of which the most memorable was his *Gold Cup* debut in 2008 when he steamrolled his way to victory, taking the scalp of his more fancied stablemate, *Kauto Star*. For the next three years, ***Denman*** put in every effort in a bid to win the *Gold Cup* for a second time, but on every occasion, he found one too good. In 2009, he finished behind *Kauto Star* for the only time at a Cheltenham Festival, his adversary gaining revenge in no uncertain terms, winning by 13 lengths. ***Denman*** finished runner-up in the next two *Gold Cup* renewals, behind the *Nigel Twiston-Davies* trained *Imperial Commander* in 2010 and the six year old, *Long Run* in 2011.

Alongside ***Denman***, two other of **Presenting**'s progeny have managed to claim two Cheltenham Festival victories, these being ***Weapon's Amnesty*** (2009 *Spa Novices' Hurdle* and the 2010 *RSA*

Chase) and most recently, ***Yorkhill***, who having won the 2016 *Neptune Investment Management Novices' Hurdle*, followed up at last season's festival by getting the better of *Top Notch* and securing victory in the *JLT Novices' Chase* by one length. ***Yorkhill*** was the solitary winner for **Presenting**'s progeny at the 2017 Cheltenham Festival and it was interesting to hear jockey *Ruby Walsh*'s post-race comments, "There has been a lot of toing and froing about whether we stay hurdling or go chasing but, to me, ***Yorkhill*** has *Gold Cup* written all over him and always has. People criticise his jumping, but he has a huge kink in him. People never realised the job *Paul Nicholls* did with ***Denman***, because he was the same. He had a kink too and they are two chestnut **Presenting**s. The best ones always do. ***Yorkhill*** has a massive engine."

The *Gold Cup* has remained tantalisingly out of reach for trainer *Willie Mullins*, and ***Yorkhill*** won't be winning it for him, at least not in the 2018 renewal, as the trainer withdrew him from the entries following a bitterly disappointing performance in the three mile *Grade 1 Leopardstown Christmas Chase* on 28th December 2017. ***Yorkhill*** was running well and two lengths clear at halfway, but it all went wrong in the second half of the race, as he started to take some chances at the fences. Despite veering badly left five out, the 7/2 chance was still tracking the leader until he weakened two from home to eventually finish eighth. This was the second disappointing performance from ***Yorkhill*** since his Cheltenham Festival victory in March. At *Fairyhouse* in April 2017, in the *Ryanair Gold Cup Novice Chase*, ***Yorkhill*** showed all his quirkiness in a wayward performance to leave *Willie Mullins* very downbeat. The 4/7 favourite had thrown away victory by hitting some fences, jumping violently to the left, almost refusing at the last having nearly gone through the wing of it, before rallying to finish close to the eventual winner, *Road to Respect*.

At the time of writing, there is still a big question mark in which festival race, ***Yorkhill*** will run, as he is currently a possible entry in *Ryanair Chase*, the *Betway Queen Mother Champion Chase* and the *Stan James Champion Hurdle Challenge Trophy*. Personally, if I was holding an ante-post betting slip on ***Yorkhill*** for the 2018 *Betway Queen Mother Champion Chase* or the *Stan James Champion Hurdle Challenge Trophy*, I would be a little concerned. The fact is that in 21 attempts, **Presenting**'s progeny have never won a two mile festival event over fences or hurdles. Indeed, in twelve attempts at the minimum distance over the larger obstacles, the offspring have so far failed to even record a place position. Admittedly, **Presenting** bred runners have fared better in the two mile hurdle category. The closest that the offspring have come to victory was way back in 2004, when ***War Of Attrition*** at 33/1 finished 2nd and just a neck behind *Brave Inca* in the *Letheby & Christopher Supreme Novices' Hurdle*. Six years later, ***Dunguib*** tried his luck in the 2010 renewal of the *Supreme*, but despite starting as the red hot 4/5 odds on favourite, he could only finish 3rd behind *Menorah* who finished a head in front of *Get Me Out Of Here*. ***Cockney Trucker*** also managed to record place dividends in the 2009 and 2011 *Vincent O'Brien County Handicap Hurdle*, which means that from a total of nine festival two mile hurdle races, **Presenting**'s progeny have finished outside the places on five occasions.

In my opinion, ***Yorkhill***'s best chance of success is in the *Ryanair Chase* within the 2½m chase category. Over the past decade, backing **Presenting**'s progeny blind in 2½ mile chases would have produced a £10.93 profit to a £1.00 each-way stake, with punters being rewarded with at least a place dividend for one in every three runs. And **Presenting**'s offspring have already registered two place positions in the *Ryanair Chase* with ***First Lieutenant*** (2/1 favourite) finishing runner-up to *Cue Card* in the 2103 renewal and ***Rajdhani Express*** securing a third place finish at odds of 18/1 in 2014. Despite his quirkiness, ***Yorkhill*** has won 2 out of 2 at Cheltenham. Indeed, of the 20 horses sired by **Presenting** that ran at last season's Cheltenham Festival, ***Yorkhill*** was the solitary winner, just as he was at the 2016 Cheltenham Festival. In fact, **Presenting**'s progeny has provided just one winner at the past five festivals, with ***Yorkhill***'s two wins being preceded by ***Rajdhani Express*** (2013), ***Present View*** (2014) and ***Call The Cops*** (2015). ***Yorkhill***'s success in the 2017 *JLT Novices' Chase* means that three of the past five Cheltenham Festival victories for **Presenting**'s offspring, have occurred in chases within the 2½ mile chase category, as both ***Rajdhani Express*** and ***Present View*** were triumphant in the *Rewards4Racing Novices' Handicap Chase* run over 2m4½.

I have already highlighted the fact that **Presenting** bred horses have performed poorly in the festival's two mile chases, and the offspring's record within the 4m chase category is only marginally better. Preceding ***Haymount***'s run in last season's *JT McNamara National Hunt Challenge Cup Amateur Riders' Novices' Chase*, where the 33/1 outsider stayed on really well after the last to claim 3rd place, only the *John P McManus* owned and *Enda Bolger* trained, ***Drombeag***, has managed to give **Presenting** supporters a pay-out in the festivals' four mile chases. In 2004, ***Drombeag*** was a one-paced 3rd in the *134th Year of National Hunt Chase Challenge Cup* and then filled the same position five years later in the 2009 3m6f *Glenfarclas Handicap Chase Cross Country Chase*. Combining the festival record of **Presenting**'s representatives in the shortest and longest chase events at the festival has therefore resulted in just three 3rd places in a total of 32 appearances.

In the 3m chase category, **Presenting**'s stock has a much better Cheltenham Festival record. In the past decade, 50 **Presenting** bred runners have lined up in three mile chases at the festival resulting in 4 winners and 9 places. Backing all fifty runners blind would have provided a profit of £11.40 to a £1.00 each-way stake. Unfortunately, **Presenting**'s progeny are likely to be absent from this year's *Gold Cup*, which is a shame as in the 12 appearances to date, the offspring have recorded two victories and five place positions. More pointedly, every **Presenting** bred runner that has lined up in the race at odds of 16/1 or under, has finished either 1st or 2nd in the race. ***War Of Attrition*** was the offspring's first *Gold Cup* contender in 2006, when victorious at odds of 15/2, which was followed by ***Denman***'s victory at 9/4, before runner up spots at 4/1, 7/1 and 8/1. And it was in 2014 when *Willie Mullins* came closest to winning the *Gold Cup*, when ***On His Own*** at 16/1, failed by just a short head to peg back winner, *Lord Windermere*.

If you are inclined to bet on outsiders, my strong recommendation is to steer clear of **Presenting**'s offspring at the Cheltenham Festival hurdle events. Over the past decade, 39 of the progeny have lined up in the festival's hurdle races at odds of 10/1 or greater and not one has managed to finish in the first three. In those 39 runs, punters would have been rewarded just twice by virtue of a couple of 4th place finishes in big field handicaps, these being ***The Sliotar*** in the 2009 *Pertemps Final* and ***Cockney Trucker*** in the 2011 *Vincent O'Brien County Handicap Hurdle*. Conversely, the record of **Presenting** bred entries towards the front of the betting market in festival hurdle races tells a completely different story. Of the 13 runners that have been sent off at single figure odds, four have won and four have been placed which equates to a 31% win ratio and a 61% win & place ratio. Placing a £1.00 each-way bet on all 13 shorter priced **Presenting** sired hurdle race entries, would have delivered a very welcome profit of £23.59.

A strategy of betting on every **Presenting** sired runner over the past four festivals would have resulted in a loss every year, with a £1.00 each-way stake at the 2017 Cheltenham Festival leaving one out of pocket by £24.10, this being a marginal improvement to the losses that would have resulted at the festivals of 2015 (minus £28.55) and 2016 (minus £33.90). Consequently, supporters of **Presenting**'s stock need to be selective if they are to make a profit.

With the larger obstacles, the offspring have a profitable track record in the 2½ mile category and punters may wish to pay special attention to the last race on the Tuesday, this being the *Close Brothers Novices' Handicap Chase*. **Presenting**'s offspring has been represented in this particular event on 12 occasions, registering two victories and three place dividends. In chases of around three miles, two races stand out, these being Friday's *Timico Cheltenham Gold Cup Chase* where the progeny have recorded 2 wins and 5 places in 12 attempts, and the *RSA Steeple Chase* on Wednesday with performance statistics from the 12 appearances of 2 wins and 3 places. Over hurdles, there is a simple rule. Back runners sired by **Presenting** provided the betting market has determined they should line up at single figure odds. 10/1 or greater – ignore them.

We may mourn the loss of **Presenting**, but having covered a total of well over 200 mares since the start of 2015, his progeny will still be seen at Cheltenham Festivals for a long time yet. Gone but not forgotten. Rest in peace **Presenting**.

Robin Des Champs (FR)

Quote from the 2017 Cheltenham Festival Stallion Guide - "Supporters can be forgiven for deciding a 'no bet' where the odds are 40/1 or more, and potentially in Wednesday's *Weatherbys Champion Bumper*. Outside of these circumstances, for every five **Robin Des Champs** sired horses that have faced the starter in a festival event, two of them crossed the winning line in first place. That is some statistic."

Robin Des Champs (21-y-o)							
Race Format	*Miles*	*Won*	*Placed*	*Unplaced*	*Total*	*Win %*	*Place %*
Hurdles	About 2m	1	0	6	7	14%	14%
	About 2m 4f	7	0	6	13	54%	54%
	About 3m	0	1	4	5	0%	20%
Chases	About 2m	0	0	1	1	0%	0%
	About 2m 4f	3	0	2	5	60%	60%
	About 3m	2	1	3	6	33%	50%
	About 4m	0	0	1	1	0%	0%
Bumper	About 2m	0	0	5	5	0%	0%
Total	**2008-2017**	**13**	**2**	**28**	**43**	**30%**	**35%**

A week before the start of last year's festival, I sent an email to a friend of mine who works for the company that for the past four years has sponsored the *Cleeve Hurdle*, a Grade 2 race over a distance of three miles, which takes place at Cheltenham racecourse in late January. In the email, I wrote, "Just a quick tip for Cheltenham. Three of the last seven winners of the *Ultima Handicap Chase* – Tuesday's 3rd race – had previously contested the *galliardhomes.com Cleeve Hurdle*! In the current list of entries for the *Ultima*, three horses - ***Un Temps Pour Tout***, *The Young Master* and *Henri Parry Morgan* - contested the *Cleeve Hurdle* – their odds range from 12/1 to 20/1. Of the three, my fancy is ***Un Temps Pour Tout***". When the **Robin Des Champs** sired ***Un Temps Pour Tout*** (9/1) had narrowly headed *Singlefarmpayment* to win the *Ultima Handicap Chase* for the second year in a row, I called him to see if he had taken my advice. "I got caught up in other things. Too busy. Did it win"? An opportunity missed!

By winning the race, the *David Pipe* trained, ***Un Temps Pour Tout***, ensured that **Robin Des Champs**' progeny have had at least one winner at every Cheltenham Festival going back to 2009. Four more **Robin Des Champs** bred horses were to appear at last year's meeting and on paper, three of them had a reasonable chance of adding to the victory of ***Un Temps Pour Tout***, or if not, potentially being placed. Next to appear was ***Champers On Ice*** who at 7/1 was 4th in the betting as the runners lined up in the *JT McNamara National Hunt Challenge Cup Amateur Riders' Novices Chase*. The seven year old hailed from the same yard as ***Un Temps Pour Tout***, and *David Pipe* had decided to fit a tongue-tie to his runner. It may have been the tongue-tie, the cheekpieces being back on, or some other reason, but ***Champers On Ice*** jumped poorly at the rear of the field and was pulled up when tailed off in the race.

The opening day's final race was the *Close Brothers Novices' Handicap Chase*, in which the third of **Robin Des Champs**' offspring would make an appearance. Like ***Champers On Ice*** in the previous race, the 14/1 chance ***Sizing Tennessee***, trained by *Colin Tizzard*, ran no sort of race and was pulled up following a blunder at the 12th fence.

The last couple of **Robin Des Champs**' stock to participate at last year's festival ran in Wednesday's *Coral Cup Handicap Hurdle*. It wasn't a surprise that ***Robinshill*** was the last of those to finish in 23rd position. After all, he was one of two 100/1 rank outsiders. The other runner sired by **Robin Des Champs** in the race was the 7/2 favourite, ***Tombstone***, who hailed from *Gordon Elliott*'s stable, and who had been all the rage in the betting market in the week leading up to race. Connections clearly thought a lot of the seven year old as they were apparently planning to supplement ***Tombstone*** for the *Champion Hurdle*, only to change their minds due to being pleased with his British handicap mark. As it turned out, the favourite was hugely disappointing and jockey, *Bryan Cooper* reported that his mount was never travelling. ***Tombstone*** eventually finished in 22nd place, just one position ahead of ***Robinshill***.

Witnessing these four hugely disappointing performances at last year's meeting, the victory by ***Un Temps Pour Tout*** clearly saved the day for **Robin Des Champs**' stock. With 4 of the 5 runners lining up at odds of 14/1 or shorter in the races, one could have expected a better return than the £3.25 profit had one backed all 5 runners blind to a £1.00 each way stake. Although, blindly backing every one of the offspring to race at the festival is not a strategy that I would recommend, although doing so, is far from being ruinous. Had one placed a £1.00 win stake on all 43 of **Robin Des Champs** sired festival runners, it would have provided a profit of £9.86, whilst backing all of them each way would have resulted in a loss of £6.32. With 13 wins and an incredibly high win rate of 30%, these figures are somewhat bewildering. So what is the explanation? The main reason is that the statistics include the performances of the amazing mare, ***Quevega***, the most renowned of **Robin Des Champs**' progeny, who won the *David Nicholson Mares' Hurdle* a record six times in a row. She was the clear favourite on every occasion, her biggest price being 2/1 in 2009. For her last four victories, she was odds-on. Taking into account five more festival victories at odds of between evens and 9/2, all of them down to ***Vautour*** and ***Sir Des Champs***, and one can understand why the rewards aren't as valuable as anticipated.

The news of ***Vautour***'s death in November 2016 due to a broken foreleg, caused by what must have been a freak accident whilst out in a paddock, was incredibly sad. All three of his festival victories were hugely impressive, a six lengths success over *Josses Hill* in the 2014 *Sky Bet Supreme Novices' Hurdle;* an awe-inspiring victory by 15 lengths in the 2015 *JLT Novices' Chase*; and then running away with the *Ryanair Chase* in 2016.

I haven't gone through all the records to find out, but I do wonder if *Willie Mullins* holds the record for training the largest number of Cheltenham Festival winners sired by one stallion. With the two victories achieved by ***Sir Des Champs*** in 2011 and 2012, added to the successes of ***Quevega*** and ***Vautour***, *Willie Mullins* has trained eleven festival winners that have all been bred out of **Robin Des Champs**. Following a solitary victory from five runs in France, ***Sir Des Champs*** was sent to *Willie Mullins* stable in the autumn of 2010, where he was trained to win his next seven races, two of which were at the Cheltenham Festival. With just one run outside of France when winning at *Navan* in January 2011, **Sir Des Champs** was unexposed when lining up for his first run at Cheltenham in the 2011 *Martin Pipe Conditional Jockeys' Handicap Hurdle*, although that didn't stop him starting as the 9/2 favourite. Ridden by *Willie Mullins*' nephew, *Emmet Mullins*, ***Sir Des Champs*** finished strongly beating outsider *Son Of Flicka* by half a length. The following season, in the second running of the *Jewson Novices' Chase* over 2m4f, ***Sir Des Champs*** jumped well, travelled strongly and was very impressive when beating *Champion Court* by 4½ lengths at odds of 3/1. Returning in 2013, ***Sir Des Champs*** was entered for the *Betfred Cheltenham Gold Cup Chase* on a day when the heavens had opened, making the ground soft. The rain-softened ground may have been his undoing, but he still put in a terrific performance only to be beaten by the equally tough *Bobs Worth*.

If we look at the results of **Robin Des Champs**' stock overall, 25 of the progeny have registered 43 Cheltenham Festival runs between them. Of those 43 runs, the 13 wins and 1 of the 2 place positions are down to just four horses, all of whom have at least two festival wins to their name. This begs the question as to whether the success of **Robin Des Champs**' festival figures is purely down to a few exceptional horses. If this is true, then supporting the stallion's future festival representatives would be a costly assumption. My personal view is that provided punters are selective in their choices, the progeny is still worth following, as deeper analysis shows that 11 of the 25 of the progeny to appear at a festival have managed to record a top six finish. I have already highlighted the four of the offspring to have won at the festival; ***Quevega***, ***Vautour***, ***Sir Des Champs*** and ***Un Temps Pour Tout***. The other seven to hit a top six spot are ***Champers On Ice*** (3rd @ 20/1); ***Robins Reef*** (4th @ 25/1); ***Un Atout*** (4th @ 6/1); ***Tombstone*** (4th @ 12/1); ***Sous Les Cieux*** (5th @ 11/2); ***Welsh Shadow*** (5th @ 28/1); and ***Tour Des Champs*** (5th at 11/1). It is also worth noting that 16 of the 25 to have appeared at the festival have raced just the once. Although all sixteen have failed to register a win or a place, ten of them lined up at odds of 20/1 or greater and so could be considered as outsiders.

In conclusion, with an incredibly impressive 30% win strike rate, punters have to take serious notice of **Robin Des Champs** sired runners at the 2018 Cheltenham Festival. Historically, it has been the shorter priced representatives who have been most successful, although there are some recent signals that this may be changing. The previously highlighted ***Un Temps Pour Tout*** won the *Ultima Handicap Chase* two years running at odds of 11/1 and 9/1. And at the 2016 festival meeting, four more of the offspring's runners, at odds of 12/1 plus, recorded top six finishes. Will there be a **Robin Des Champs** bred victor at the 2018 meeting, making it 10 years on the trot for the progeny to register a Cheltenham Festival winner? I wouldn't bet against it.

Saddler Maker (IRE)

Quote from the 2017 Cheltenham Festival Stallion Guide - "It is a fantastic start for the stock of **Saddler Maker** to have already achieved five runner-up positions from just seven festival runs and if you happen to strongly fancy a **Saddler Maker** bred runner come the spring, then I would not dissuade you from placing a bet."

Saddler Maker (Died as an 18-y-o in 2016)							
Race Format	*Miles*	***Won***	***Placed***	***Unplaced***	***Total***	***Win %***	***Place %***
Hurdles	About 2m	0	2	2	4	0%	50%
	About 2m 4f	1	1	1	3	33%	67%
	About 3m	0	1	0	1	0%	100%
Chases	About 2m	0	0	0	0	-	-
	About 2m 4f	0	3	0	3	0%	100%
	About 3m	0	0	3	3	0%	0%
	About 4m	0	0	0	0	-	-
Bumper	About 2m	0	0	0	0	-	-
Total	**2008-2017**	**1**	**7**	**6**	**14**	**7%**	**57%**

We all know that the Cheltenham Festival is ultra-competitive with every runner prepared and trained to be in the best condition possible to succeed. If you are lucky enough to go to the festival meetings, the easy bit is having a fantastic time there. What is much more difficult is picking winners and making a profit, and this Guide attempts to make that job slightly less challenging. In that regard, the stallion **Saddler Maker** is of considerable help.

Saddler Maker is the only stallion within this Guide where the statistics show that a **Saddler Maker** sired runner has a better record of finishing in the first three at a Cheltenham Festival than not doing so. Admittedly, this stallion has only been represented at the festival 14 times and in just the past three meetings. Nevertheless, it is a hugely impressive statistic. Just seven of **Saddler Maker**'s offspring are responsible for the 14 festival appearances, only two of which have so far failed to register a top 3 finish.

So how much profit would punters have made had they placed a £1.00 each way bet on every single festival runner sired by **Saddler Maker**? The answer is a measly £1.10, which taking into account this stallion's splendid festival record, is yet another clear example of how difficult it is to make a profit at Cheltenham Festivals. Clearly, the profit figure would be much larger had 2 or 3 of those seven place positions resulted in victories instead. In truth, a win rate of 7% is nothing to write home about. What is notable is that **Saddler Maker**'s offspring have finished in 2nd or 3rd position for one in every two festival runs.

It is worth noting that the stallion's festival representatives are usually towards the front end of the market, albeit rarely in the front 2 or 3 in the betting. Indeed, for 10 of the 14 festival appearances, the **Saddler Maker** bred runners have lined up at starting prices falling between 8/1 and 16/1. The three runs at shorter odds have been at 7/2, 4/1 and 6/1, and there has only one appearance from the offspring at greater than 16/1, when ***Label Des Obeaux*** finished 12th in the 2016 *Martin Pipe Conditional Jockeys' Handicap Hurdle* at a price of 25/1.

The shortest priced festival appearance of **Saddler Maker**'s stock was from ***Apple's Jade***, who was the third favourite at 7/2 in last year's highly thrilling *OLBG Mares' Hurdle*. ***Apple's Jade*** was up against two top class mares from *Willie Mullins' Closutton* stables, *Limini* (6/4F) and *Vroum Vroum Mag* (11/4) who had both won at the 2016 Cheltenham Festival. Trainer *Gordon Elliott* had fitted ***Apple's Jade*** with a first-time tongue-tie for the race and whether that helped or not, who knows, but the mare ran exceptionally well, rallying gamely after being headed at the last to win by 1½ lengths from *Vroum Vroum Mag*. ***Apple Jade***'s first festival run, when she was trained by *Willie Mullins*, was in the 2016 *JCB Triumph Hurdle*, when she claimed the runner-up spot at a price of 12/1 behind the winner, *Ivanovich Gorbatov*. At the 2018 Cheltenham Festival, there is a very strong possibility that we will witness for the first time, a **Saddler Maker** sired runner being an odds-on favourite. At the time of writing, ***Apple's Jade*** is the 8/13 favourite for a repeat win in the 2018 renewal of the *OLBG Mares' Hurdle*.

The very first **Saddler Maker** bred runner to appear at a Cheltenham Festival was ***Bouvreuil*** who was the sole representative of the offspring at the 2015 meeting, where he finished runner-up in the *Fred Winter Juvenile Handicap Hurdle*, at a starting price of 14/1. It was a very satisfactory race for *Paul Nicholls*, who trained both ***Bouvreuil*** and the winner, *Qualando*, rewarding exacta backers of these two horses, with a dividend of £481.40. The following year, ***Bouvreuil*** was entered in the listed *Close Brothers Novices' Handicap Chase*, where *Paul Nicholls* was attempting to emulate his one and only success in this event, when seven years previously, his stable's *Chapoturgeon* became the only five year old to win the race. When ***Bouvreuil*** took a narrow advantage at the last, it looked as though the 14/1 shot may be the second five year old winner, but his 9 year old rival, *Ballyalton*, rallied and regained the lead in the final 120 yards to leave ***Bouvreuil*** to finish with a runner-up spot for the second year in a row.

Paul Nicholls was no doubt hoping it would be third time lucky at the 2017 Cheltenham Festival when ***Bouvreuil***, who was now in the ownership of *John P McManus*, made his third festival appearance in the Grade 3 *Brown Advisory & Merriebelle Stable Plate Handicap Chase*. Although he didn't win, it was another sound performance from ***Bouvreuil*** who was no match for *Road To Respect*, the comfortable winner, and the 10/1 chance came home in 3rd place at a price of 10/1. There aren't too many racehorses as young as seven years old that have already achieved three Cheltenham Festival top three finishes.

I advised earlier that of the seven of **Saddler Maker**'s offspring to have raced at the festival, five of them have registered a top three finish. ***Bouvreuil*** has achieved it three times, ***Apple's Jade*** twice, and ***Bristol De Mai***, ***Alpha Des Obeaux*** and ***Messire Des Obeaux*** once. ***Bristol De Mai*** was one of three 4/1 co-favourites, when finishing 2nd and some 3 lengths adrift of the winner, *Black Hercules*, in the 2016 *JLT Novices Chase*. Last year, ***Bristol De Mai*** went for the big one, the *Timico Cheltenham Gold Cup Chase* and at six years old, he was the youngest horse to line up. He performed reasonably well, albeit that he made a number of jumping errors towards the end of the race. He finished in 7th place at a price of 16/1.

It was also at the 2016 meeting when ***Alpha Des Obeaux*** achieved his festival runner-up position. He ran really well to finish some 7 lengths behind the incredibly impressive *Thistlecrack* in the 2016 *Ryanair World Hurdle*. ***Alpha Des Obeaux*** also made an appearance at the 2017 Cheltenham Festival, when trainer *Mouse Morris*, entered him to race in the *RSA Novices' Chase*. In a competitive affair, ***Alpha Des Obeaux*** finished some 18 lengths off the leading pair to take 4th place at a price of 6/1. He may have done better had he not broken a blood vessel.

Having finished 7th in the 2016 *Fred Winter Juvenile Handicap Hurdle*, ***Messire Des Obeaux*** returned twelve months later to finish 3rd in the *Neptune Investment Management Novices' Hurdle*. At a price of 8/1, ***Messire Des Obeaux*** ran on well up the Cheltenham Hill but was unable to match the pace of the front two.

Delving deeper into the festival results of **Saddler Maker** sired runners reveals a pattern that we should perhaps keep an eye upon to see if the trend continues, albeit this insight should perhaps be viewed with some scepticism, as with just 14 runs on board, it is so easy to put two and two together to make five. However, **Saddler Maker**'s progeny have so far managed to achieve five top three finishes in six festival events over a distance of 2½ miles, making the middle distance by far the most profitable for punters to follow. It is worth noting that the one failure at 2½ miles was courtesy of the previously mentioned ***Label Des Obeaux***, who at 25/1, has been the sole **Saddler Maker** sired representative to line up in a festival race at a price of greater than 16/1.

Just seven of **Saddler Maker**'s progeny have raced at the past three festival meetings. And what a start with one win and seven places from just 14 runs. Unless there is a sudden deterioration in the offspring's performances, then **Saddler Maker** is definitely a stallion to follow at Cheltenham Festivals.

Saint Des Saints (FR)

Quote from the 2017 Cheltenham Festival Stallion Guide - "If we look at the festival performances of all 24 **Saint Des Saints** sired runners, then the obvious conclusion is that, for the most part, the progeny acquit themselves well at Cheltenham Festivals, as indicated by 62.5% of the runners attaining a top six position and a 42% win and place strike rate."

Saint Des Saints (20-y-o)							
Race Format	*Miles*	***Won***	***Placed***	***Unplaced***	***Total***	***Win %***	***Place %***
Hurdles	About 2m	0	4	2	6	0%	67%
	About 2m 4f	1	0	3	4	25%	25%
	About 3m	0	0	2	2	0%	0%
Chases	About 2m	0	0	1	1	0%	0%
	About 2m 4f	1	0	2	3	33%	33%
	About 3m	0	3	6	9	0%	33%
	About 4m	0	0	0	0	-	-
Bumper	About 2m	0	1	1	2	0%	50%
Total	**2008-2017**	**2**	**8**	**17**	**27**	**7%**	**37%**

Having achieved six place dividends and a victory from thirteen runners at the previous two meetings, the 2017 Cheltenham Festival turned out to be damp squib for supporters of **Saint Des Saints**' offspring. Only three **Saint Des Saints** sired runners made an appearance at last year's meeting and all three were unplaced.

The highest rated of **Saint Des Saints**' progeny is the *Susannah Ricci* owned ***Djakadam*** and setting off as the 3/1 favourite in the 2017 *Timico Cheltenham Gold Cup Chase*, many pundits believed that ***Djakadam*** had a great chance of lifting the trophy in what would be the eight year old's third attempt in the race. I must admit, I thought otherwise. The runners that take part in a *Gold Cup* have been prepared and trained to be in tip-top condition, and competing in the heat of this prestigious race takes a lot out of a horse. If a horse is beaten on his first attempt in the race, my suspicion is that to have the horse in the same peak condition as when he was beaten previously is incredibly difficult to achieve. It is when the pressure is on in a *Gold Cup* for the second time around, that the battle scars from earlier encounters are likely to be felt. My hypothesis is supported by the statistics. This century, 66 runners that were beaten on their *Gold Cup* debut have tried again and all of them have been beaten. The last horse to have won a *Gold Cup*, having been beaten on their first attempt, was *See More Business* in 1999. And for those with long memories, *See More Business* hardly had a race in the 1998 renewal, being carried out by *Cyborgo* barely a third of the way into the race.

In the 2017 *Timico Cheltenham Gold Cup Chase*, ***Djakadam*** was travelling well and was running a perfect race until push came to shove towards the end of the race. Making a mistake at the second last, ***Djakadam*** was soon headed by *Sizing John*, the eventual winner, and then tired with no extra to give as they approached the line. ***Djakadam*** finished 4th, just outside the places. In my view, ***Djakadam***'s best chance of winning the big prize was in his first attempt in 2015. He ran well to finish runner-up to the novice, *Coneygree*, who put in a brilliant jumping display, virtually leading throughout. The following year, ***Djakadam*** again found one too good, finishing second this time to *Don Cossack* who looked all over the winner once *Cue Card* had fallen three from home.

Another of **Saint Des Saints**' offspring attempting to improve on his 2016 festival performance was the *Philip Hobbs* trained, ***Wait For Me***. In the 2016 *Vincent O'Brien County Handicap Hurdle*, ***Wait For Me*** lined up as the 7/1 joint favourite and ran well to finish 4th and a head behind his stablemate, *Sternrubin*. In the 2017 running of the race, now named the *Randox Health County Handicap Hurdle*, ***Wait For Me*** could only finish in 9th, although he was actually a lot closer to the winner than in the 2016 contest. In 2017, ***Wait For Me*** finished 4½ lengths behind the victor whereas, despite picking up a place dividend in the 2016 renewal, he was over six lengths away from first past the post, *Superb Story*.

Unlike ***Djakadam*** and ***Wait For Me***, the other **Saint Des Saints** sired representative last season was making his debut at the Festival, and ***Balbir Du Mathan*** performed pretty much as his starting price would suggest. The 50/1 chance was pulled up in the *Fulke Walwyn Kim Muir Challenge Cup Amateur Riders' Handicap Chase*.

Although there were only three **Saint Des Saints** sired runners at the last meeting, who were all unable to add to the stock's win and place statistics, the stallion's festival record overall is still better than most others. Of the fifteen of the progeny that have appeared at the Cheltenham Festival, eight of them are responsible for the two wins and eight place positions. It is due to the slightly disappointing 7% win rate that had one backed all 27 of **Saints Des Saints**' festival runners blind to a £1.00 each-way stake, only a small profit of £3.18 would have resulted. Nevertheless a profit is still a profit and I am still very interested in a stallion where over half of the offspring have delivered at least a festival placing. In addition, a 37% win and place strike rate translates into collecting some winnings for better than one in every three of the progeny's appearances.

Both of the festival victories for **Saint Des Saints**' offspring were achieved in races over a distance of around 2½ miles, the first of which was in the 2012 *Byrne Group Plate*, where ***Salut Flo*** was backed into favouritism to win at odds of 9/2. Three years later and the 9/1 shot, ***Aux Ptits Soins***, trained by *Paul Nicholls* just held on in a tight finish to win the 2015 *Coral Cup*. If you are a fan of quirky trends, then a win is therefore due in 2018; a **Saints Des Saints** sired festival winner every three years!

With just 27 festival runs spread across the seven race categories, it is difficult to draw any concrete conclusions about specific race types as any analysis is based upon a small number of results within any given category. Nevertheless, I still believe it is worth highlighting the four festival performances of the **Saints Des Saints** sired four year olds, as three of the progeny secured places and all at rewarding prices. Strangely enough, it was the horse who lined up with the shortest price of the four representatives who failed to secure a place, the *Paul Nicholls* trained ***Connetable***, who at a price of 14/1, finished 11th in the 2016 *JCB Triumph Hurdle*. *Paul Nicholls* was also the trainer of ***Sametegal***, the only other **Saints Des Saints** bred runner to appear in the *Triumph Hurdle*. In the 2013 running, at a price of 33/1, ***Sametegal*** secured third position behind stablemate *Far West* who finished runner-up behind the runaway winner, *Our Conor*.

Paul Nicholls has a great record with his four year old festival entries, especially in the *Fred Winter Juvenile Handicap Hurdle*, where he has trained three of the last eight winners. In the 2015 running of the contest, *Paul Nicholls* saddled both *Qualando* and *Bouvreuil* who finished 1st and 2nd respectively. Behind the *Ditcheat* trained duo was the **Saint Des Saints** sired, ***The Saint James***, who finished 3rd at a price of 33/1. With odds for the 1-2-3 of 25/1, 14/1 and 33/1, the Trifecta dividend was £13,942.60! *Paul Nicholls* was at it again in the 2016 *Fred Winter*, securing a 1-2 for the second year in a row when stablemates *Diego Du Charmil* and ***Romain De Senam*** fought out a tight finish. It was so very close to being a winner for the **Saint Des Saints** bred ***Romain De Senam*** (20/1), who ran on really strongly in the last 100 yards, just failing to catch *Diego Du Charmil* by a head. One or two more yards and ***Romain De Senam*** would have won.

We should no doubt be cautious about making any foolhardy conclusions based upon the results of just four runs, but with three place positions secured at prices of 20/1, 33/1 and 33/1, I will certainly be one of the punters willing to risk a small each-way bet on any **Saints Des Saints** bred four year old who is declared for the 2018 Cheltenham Festival. And should the **Saint Des Saints** sired four year old hail from *Paul Nicholl's Ditcheat* yard and be declared for the *Boodles Fred Winter Juvenile Handicap Hurdle*, then perhaps my bet will be considerably larger.

I am a huge fan of **Saint Des Saints**' offspring. Sixteen top six finishes inclusive of two wins and eight place dividends from just 27 festival appearances says everything. Even though there was no return from last year's three runners, the evidence overall suggests that punters will be rewarded by supporting the progeny's runners. Being named **Saint Des Saints**, what can one say other than keep the faith!

Shantou (USA)

Quote from the 2017 Cheltenham Festival Stallion Guide - "The data is beyond question. Punters will make a profit betting on **Shantou**'s offspring at Cheltenham Festivals."

Shantou (25-y-o)								
Race Format	*Miles*	***Won***	***Placed***	***Unplaced***	***Total***	***Win %***	***Place %***
Hurdles	About 2m	0	0	4	4	0%	0%
	About 2m 4f	0	2	2	4	0%	50%
	About 3m	0	2	7	9	0%	22%
Chases	About 2m	0	0	0	0	-	-
	About 2m 4f	2	0	4	6	33%	33%
	About 3m	0	4	2	6	0%	67%
	About 4m	0	1	2	3	0%	33%
Bumper	About 2m	1	0	0	1	100%	100%
Total	**2008-2017**	**3**	**9**	**21**	**33**	**9%**	**36%**

In this Guide's Introduction, I write "There is compelling evidence that a horse's breeding is a critical factor when it comes to picking winners. The progeny of some stallions perform creditably at the festival time and time again, whereas others consistently struggle". **Shantou** is a classic example of a stallion whose offspring perform at Cheltenham Festivals year after year.

If we take the festival results of **Shantou**'s stock overall, 23 of the progeny have registered 34 runs between them with all bar one of the appearances taking place within the past decade. Of the 23 of the progeny that have tackled the Cheltenham Festival, nine of them, almost 40%, have managed a top three finish. From a financial perspective, with three wins and 9 place positions on the board from 34 festival appearances, blindly backing all of **Shantou**'s runners at £1.00 each way would have produced a handsome profit of £47.68. And with **Shantou**, it is not a roller-coaster of big profits one year and then losses the next. This particular stallion delivers a consistent profit year after year. A strategy of blindly backing every **Shantou** bred runner at level stakes has been rewarded with a profit at the past five Cheltenham Festivals. For the record, to a £1.00 each-way stake, the returns have been as follows; 2013 - £28.38; 2014 - £7.80; 2015 - £2.20; 2016 - £3.80; 2017 - £11.50.

Nine of **Shantou**'s offspring lined up at the 2017 Cheltenham Festival, four of them taking part in hurdle events and the remaining five racing over the larger obstacles. Beginning with the hurdle races, ***Death Duty***, out of *Gordon Elliott*'s yard, was all the rage in Friday's three mile *Albert Bartlett Novices' Hurdle* and started as the well backed 13/8 favourite. Unbeaten in four novice hurdles, many anticipated that the six year old would become the first of **Shantou**'s stock to win a Cheltenham Festival hurdle event. But it wasn't to be. ***Death Duty*** was well beaten, his stamina giving way prior to unseating jockey *Bryan Cooper* at the last.

Death Duty was one of two **Shantou** bred runners to appear in a three mile hurdle event at last year's festival. The stallion's second representative, ***The Tourard Man***, was to race in Thursday's Listed *Pertemps Network Final Handicap Hurdle*. Trained by *Alan King*, it was ***The Tourard Man***'s second visit to the festival and his second appearance in this event, having finished 3rd at 20/1 in the 2015 renewal. This time round, in 2017, ***The Tourard Man*** was now considered a veteran at eleven years old and lined up in the race as one of two unfancied 66/1 rank outsiders. Despite taking a while to settle in the race, he made headway two out and stayed on to reward each-way backers with a 4th place dividend. Even though **Shantou**'s progeny are yet to win a hurdle contest in a total of 18 attempts, the four place positions have been at rather rewarding SPs of 9/1, 20/1, 50/1 and 66/1.

The 50/1 outsider, trained by County Kildare based, *Alan Fleming*, was ***Tully East***, who finished 4th in the 2016 *Martin Pipe Conditional Jockeys' Handicap Hurdle*. After this event, *Alan Fleming* sent ***Tully East*** to race over fences, and following three runs in novice events, the horse would appear at Cheltenham for a second time in the 2017 *Close Brothers Novices' Handicap Chase* over 2m4½f. As it turned out, ***Tully East*** was given a wonderful ride by jockey *Denis O'Regan*, making smooth headway after 3 out before leading at the last and running on well up the famous Cheltenham Hill to win comfortably at 8/1. It was the second victory for **Shantou**'s progeny in the festival's 2½m chase category, the first success courtesy of ***Ballynagour*** (12/1), from *David Pipe*'s stable, who won the 2014 *Byrne Group Plate*. With these two victories over the bigger obstacles, plus five places from fifteen runs in the festival's chase events, **Shantou**'s offspring are providing punters with a return on their each-way bets for close to one in every two appearances over fences, which is an exceptional strike rate.

As we approach this year's 4-day extravaganza at Cheltenham, and you are dissecting the form and looking through the long list of festival entries, make sure you keep your eyes open for any runner sired by **Shantou**, and then bear in mind the following when determining your bets:

£47.68 profit in backing to a £1.00 each way stake all 34 of **Shantou**'s festival runners
A profit every year for the past five festivals in backing **Shantou**'s offspring blind to level stakes
9 out of 23 of the progeny to race at festival meetings have secured a top three finish
7 out of 15 runs in chase events has resulted in rewards (2 wins and 5 places)
4 places achieved from 18 runs in hurdle events with SPs of 9/1, 20/1, 50/1 and 66/1
1 win from 1 run in the Bumper (***Briar Hill*** @ 25/1 in the 2013 *Weatherbys Champion Bumper*)

As the meerkats say in those adverts – Simples!

Shirocco (GER)

Quote from the 2017 Cheltenham Festival Stallion Guide - "A 30% win strike rate is a hugely encouraging statistic for this young stallion, as is the £14.50 profit to a £1.00 win stake had one backed all ten of the offspring's festival runs to date. It is still early days to make any ultra-confident predictions about **Shirocco** sired festival runners, but my expectation is that punters will continue to be rewarded by backing them."

Shirocco (17-y-o)							
Race Format	*Miles*	*Won*	*Placed*	*Unplaced*	*Total*	*Win %*	*Place %*
Hurdles	About 2m	2	0	1	3	67%	67%
	About 2m 4f	0	0	6	6	0%	0%
	About 3m	0	1	0	1	0%	100%
Chases	About 2m	0	0	0	0	-	-
	About 2m 4f	0	0	0	0	-	-
	About 3m	0	1	0	1	0%	100%
	About 4m	1	0	0	1	100%	100%
Bumper	About 2m	0	0	0	0	-	-
Total	**2008-2017**	**3**	**2**	**7**	**12**	**25%**	**42%**

There were only two runners sired by **Shirocco** at last year's Cheltenham Festival which leaves us with a total of just 12 festival appearances from the stallion's offspring upon which to identify any trends and conclusions. Any analysis is made all the harder as just three of the progeny are responsible for nine of those 12 festival appearances. Three other **Shirocco** sired horses have only one festival appearance to their name and all three performances were very disappointing.

The *Jonjo O'Neill* trained ***Minella Rocco*** has been to the Cheltenham Festival twice, one of which was last year when the *JP McManus* owned runner was entered for the *Timico Cheltenham Gold Cup Chase*. The same owner/trainer combination had been successful five years earlier in the 2012 *Betfred Cheltenham Gold Cup Chase* when *Synchronised* under a determined ride by jockey *Tony McCoy* prevailed to win by 2¼ lengths from 50/1 outsider, *The Giant Bolster*. In the 2017 renewal of this prestigious event, the *McManus/O'Neill* duo had to settle for a runner-up slot. In truth, ***Minella Rocco***, was a touch outpaced when the pace of the race started to increase and the **Shirocco** sired 18/1 chance was in seventh place as they jumped the second last. Nevertheless, from that point on, he stayed on strongly and snatched second place in the dying strides from *Native River*. ***Minella Rocco*** never threatened the winner, *Sizing John*, who stayed on well up the Cheltenham Hill and won by 2¾ lengths. ***Minella Rocco*** had finished in front of *Native River* previously at the 2016 festival meeting, this time when he was victorious in winning the *146th Year Of The National Hunt Chase Challenge Cup*. Given a cracking ride by amateur jockey, *Derek O'Connor*, ***Minella Rocco*** made headway four out, led before the last and stayed on well to beat *Native River* by 1¼ lengths. In winning this 4m chase, ***Minella Rocco*** became the 3rd of **Shirocco**'s stock to become a Cheltenham Festival winner.

About 90 minutes before ***Minella Rocco***'s victory, ***Annie Power*** had provided the second festival victory for **Shirocco**'s offspring, when taking the 2016 *Stan James Champion Hurdle Challenge Trophy*. **Annie Power** had been supplemented for the festival's showpiece hurdle event just the week before, and for owner *Susannah Ricci*, it was third time lucky as the 5/2 favourite made all and drew clear at the last to win impressively from *My Tent Or Yours*. In winning the *Champion Hurdle*, ***Annie Power*** became the first mare to be successful in this event since *Flakey Dove* in 1994.

Annie Power is now retired, having won 15 of her 17 starts. Her two defeats occurred at the Cheltenham Festival in 2014 and 2015. ***Annie Power*** made her festival debut in the 2014 *Ladbrokes World Hurdle* and when jockey *Ruby Walsh* was level with the *Barry Geraghty* ridden, *More Of That*, just before the last hurdle, many would have expected the 11/8 favourite to quicken away and win. But, it wasn't to be, and *More Of That* stayed on the better to win by 1½ lengths. It was ***Annie Power***'s only start over three miles and the only time she would be beaten when completing a race. The following year, she famously fell at the last in the *OLBG Mares' Hurdle* with the race at her mercy and saving the bookmakers millions of pounds after her trainer *Willie Mullins* had already been successful with *Douvan, Un De Sceaux* and *Faugheen* earlier in the day.

The one other **Shirocco** sired horse to appear at a Cheltenham Festival more than once is the *Paul Nicholls* trained, ***Lac Fontana***, who was making his 4th appearance last season in the *Martin Pipe Conditional Jockeys' Handicap Hurdle*. In the race over a distance of 2m4½f, ***Lac Fontana*** struggled to make any impression, weakening three from home and finishing down the field in 16th position. His performance in the *Vincent O'Brien County Handicap Hurdle* three years earlier was rather different, a race he won when rallying two from home and running on strongly up the hill to get up on the line and win at a price of 11/1. In the previous festival of 2013, ***Lac Fontana*** became the very first of **Shirocco**'s brood to make an appearance at a Cheltenham Festival when, at 25/1, he finished 8th in the *JCB Triumph Hurdle*. His third festival appearance was in 2015, after his triumph in the *County Hurdle*, where in another highly competitive contest, the *Coral Cup*, he ran disappointingly to finish ninth.

The three **Shirocco** sired horses to have only made one appearance at a festival have all disappointed. In 2014, the *David Pipe* trained ***Red Sherlock***, lined up in the *Neptune Investment Management Novices' Hurdle* as the 7/2 second favourite. As it turned out, he weakened coming up the hill and eventually finished ninth, being no match for the winning favourite, *Faugheen*. In the 2015 Coral Cup, ***Mijhaar*** took part in the same race as ***Lac Fontana***, but finished four places further back in 13th. And in the 2016 renewal of the *Coral Cup*, the *Philip Hobbs* trained ***Rock The Kasbah*** went off as the 15/2 favourite, but he ran abysmally coming home in 22nd out of the 26 runners who set off.

Annie Power aside, who would have won the 2015 *OLBG Mares' Hurdle* had she not fallen at the last hurdle, it is worth noting that the other five festival runs within the 2½m category have all been hugely disappointing with no **Shirocco** sired runner finishing higher than 9th place. This is in stark contrast to the six festival performances which have not been within this category; three wins, two second places and one 8th placing. Bear in mind, however, that two of the wins and both place positions have come from just two of the offspring, ***Annie Power*** and ***Minella Rocco***.

The table above makes very good reading. Had one backed all 12 of the offspring's festival runs to date, the result would be a profit of £14.23 to a £1.00 each-way stake. And if there is anyone out there who truly believes, from just six appearances over 2½ miles, that **Shirocco** bred runners should be avoided over the middle distance trips, then betting £1.00 each-way on any distance other than 2½ miles, produces a significantly enhanced profit of £26.23. That being said, we would be foolish to ignore the very positive impact that ***Annie Power*** and ***Minella Rocco*** have had on this stallion's festival results and profits. Taking everything into account, my head says that the jury is out and I should sit on the fence. Nevertheless, with this stallion, I am inclined to be half-full rather than half-empty. My hunch is that **Shirocco**'s offspring will continue to reward punters who support them.

Sinndar (IRE)

Quote from the 2017 Cheltenham Festival Stallion Guide - "Punters should take a serious interest if they find any **Sinndar** bred runners among the list of entries in Wednesday's *Fred Winter Juvenile Novices' Handicap Hurdle* and also in Friday's opening event, the *JCB Triumph Hurdle*."

Sinndar (21-y-o)							
Race Format	Miles	Won	Placed	Unplaced	Total	Win %	Place %
Hurdles	About 2m	0	5	7	12	0%	42%
	About 2m 4f	0	0	2	2	0%	0%
	About 3m	0	1	1	2	0%	50%
Chases	About 2m	0	0	0	0	-	-
	About 2m 4f	0	0	0	0	-	-
	About 3m	0	0	0	0	-	-
	About 4m	0	0	0	0	-	-
Bumper	About 2m	0	0	1	1	0%	0%
Total	**2008-2017**	**0**	**6**	**11**	**17**	**0%**	**35%**

Although there have only been 17 runs from **Sinndar**'s offspring at the Cheltenham Festival, eight of those runs have taken place in the festival's juvenile hurdle events for four year olds, these being the *Triumph Hurdle* and the *Fred Winter*. At last year's meeting, there were only two **Sinndar** sired representatives at the festival, one of which was the four year old ***Project Bluebook***, trained by *John Quinn*, who rewarded each-way backers by securing 4th place in the *Fred Winter Juvenile Handicap Hurdle* at a price of 14/1. Five years previous in the 2012 renewal, another **Sinndar** bred runner also recorded a 4th place in the *Fred Winter*, ***Kazilan*** at 7/1. In between these two 4th place finishes, two other of **Sinndar**'s progeny have raced in the *Fred Winter*, but both of them were less fancied in the market. ***Noble Inn*** (20/1) was placed 11th in 2014 and ***Verawal*** was a 66/1 chance when he finished 15th in the 2015 renewal.

Sinndar's offspring have an even better record in the other festival race confined to four year-olds, the *Triumph Hurdle*. Two **Sinndar** sired runners took their chance in the 2009 *JCB Triumph Hurdle* and unsurprisingly, it was the *Willie Mullins* trained ***Mourad***, who performed the better of the pair, when finishing 3rd at 14/1 ahead of ***Tyrrells Wood***, who at a price of 66/1, put in a very respectable showing to finish in 8th. Four years later in the 2013 running, *Willie Mullins* had another **Sinndar** bred runner represented in the *Triumph*, ***Diakali***, who was having his fourth run over hurdles. In the race, he led for much of way, just as he had done in his previous outing in the *Spring Juvenile Hurdle* at *Leopardstown* in February. On that occasion, he finished second as *Our Conor* powered past him to win by five lengths. In the 2013 *JCB Triumph Hurdle* it was the same story again, although *Our Conor* was even more impressive on this occasion, effortlessly passing ***Diakali*** two out and going on to win by 15 lengths. As for ***Diakali***, once he was passed by the winner, he could only keep going at the same pace and just missed out on a place dividend, finishing in 4th. In the 2015 renewal of the *Triumph*, *Nicky Henderson* trained the 1st, 2nd and 3rd in the race, with the **Sinndar** sired ***Hargam*** unsuited by the soft ground, finishing in third.

All three top 4 finishers in the **Triumph** were to race at the Cheltenham Festival again. In 2014, ***Diakali*** at a price of 25/1, finished in 4th place for the second consecutive year, but as he was racing in the *Vincent O'Brien County Handicap Hurdle* with 28 runners, on this occasion he picked up a place dividend. Two years after ***Mourad***'s 3rd in the *Triumph Hurdle*, *Willie Mullins* entered the gelding in the 2011 *Ladbrokes World Hurdle* over a distance of three miles. ***Mourad*** was 3rd favourite in the race at 8/1 and the bookies had it spot on. Favourite *Big Buck's* won the race for the 3rd consecutive year, chased home by 2nd favourite *Grand Crus*, with ***Mourad*** following the pair home to finish in third. In the 2012 renewal of the race, ***Mourad*** was to take on the winner again but to no avail. *Big Buck's* won for 4th time in a row with ***Mourad*** weakening rapidly, tailing off to finish in 6th place at 33/1. Where ***Diakali*** and ***Mourad*** managed to achieve a place position following their runs in the *Triumph Hurdle*, in comparison, ***Hargam*** has been rather disappointing. He finished last of the 10 finishers in the 2016 *Stan James Champion Hurdle Challenge Trophy* at a price of 16/1 and at last year's festival, this time at 14/1, he was never a threat when finishing well towards the back of the field in the *Coral Cup*.

Although yet to manage a festival win, or indeed a festival runner-up, **Sinndar**'s offspring have managed to achieve a 3rd or 4th placing on seven occasions. Punters need to look out for **Sinndar** sired runners that are entered in the two races confined to four year olds, these being the *Triumph Hurdle* and the *Fred Winter*. Of the eight **Sinndar** representatives to compete in these events, the quintet that were more towards the front of the betting market, all finished in third or fourth position. It goes without saying that if you come across a **Sinndar** bred entry, priced up at under 20/1, in either the 2018 *Triumph* or *Fred Winter* contests, make sure you back the runner each way.

Stowaway (GB)

Quote from the 2017 Cheltenham Festival Stallion Guide - "**Stowaway**'s brood made a blistering start in their early festival appearances, but in the past two years, there have been five rather uninspiring runs from the offspring. With that in mind, I am rather undecided on the likely success or otherwise of **Stowaway** sired runners at the 2017 Cheltenham Festival. My hunch is that, over time, the progeny will provide us with further festival successes."

Stowaway (Died as a 21-y-o in 2015)							
Race Format	*Miles*	***Won***	***Placed***	***Unplaced***	***Total***	***Win %***	***Place %***
Hurdles	About 2m	1	0	0	1	-	-
	About 2m 4f	1	1	1	3	33%	67%
	About 3m	0	0	2	2	0%	0%
Chases	About 2m	0	1	0	1	0%	100%
	About 2m 4f	0	1	2	3	0%	33%
	About 3m	0	0	2	2	0%	0%
	About 4m	0	0	0	0	-	-
Bumper	About 2m	1	0	0	1	100%	100%
Total	**2008-2017**	**3**	**3**	**7**	**13**	**23%**	**46%**

A record number of **Stowaway** sired horses appeared at the 2017 Cheltenham Festival, but it was still a relatively small number. Just four! And all four of them took their chance on the Friday, the last day of the meeting. After five relatively disappointing performances at the previous two festival meetings, 2017 was much more satisfactory for this stallion, with one victory, one place and another runner who looked likely to be in the shake up towards the end of his race before falling.

Friday's penultimate race, the *Martin Pipe Conditional Jockey's Handicap Hurdle* provided a very satisfactory outcome for trainer *Gordon Elliott* as two of his three entries for the race finished 1st and 3rd, both of whom were sired by **Stowaway**. *Gigginstown House Stud* had won the race twice in the previous eight runnings of this event with *Sir Des Champs* and *Don Poli*, and the owners made it 3 from 9 when ***Champagne Classic*** (12/1) stayed on strongly having taken the lead two out, to win by 2¼ lengths. The winner's stablemate, ***Runfordave***, kept on at the same pace up the Cheltenham Hill to secure 3rd place at a price of 9/1.

It would have been interesting to have seen where the *Tom George* trained, ***The Worlds End***, would have finished had he not fallen in the *Albert Bartlett Novices' Hurdle*. The **Stowaway** sired 10/1 chance made rapid headway three from home and was alongside the leaders and well in contention when he fell two out. We will never know if he would have won, but based on his victory at *Aintree* three weeks later in the *Doom Bar Sefton Novices' Hurdle*, in my view, he certainly would have gone close.

The fourth Stowaway contender to appear at last year's Cheltenham Festival, ***Outlander***, who has achieved the highest Official Rating of all of **Stowaway**'s stock, lined up in the *Timico Cheltenham Gold Cup Chase*. The 10/1 chance never looked comfortable in mid-division and started to be ridden not long after half-way. He eventually finished in 10th place and last of those that managed to complete the race. It was ***Outlander***'s third consecutive appearance at a Cheltenham Festival and the third time that he has disappointed. As the 4/1 second favourite, he came home in 6th position in the 2015 *Neptune Investment Management Novices' Hurdle*, and at the 2016 festival, this time at 6/1, he fell four fences from home in the *JLT Novices' Chase*.

With regard to the 46% win and place strike rate showing in **Stowaway**'s festival performance table above, there is no denying that the star of the show is ***Champagne Fever***, responsible for 50% of the progeny's win and place positions to date. ***Champagne Fever***, trained by *Willie Mullins*, was the first of **Stowaway**'s offspring to line up in a festival event, when entered for the 2012 *Weatherbys Champion Bumper*. Ridden by the trainer's son, *Patrick Mullins*, the grey gelding led from start to finish, winning the race at the rewarding odds of 16/1. The following season, ***Champagne Fever*** made it two wins from two in festival events when having made all in the *William Hill Supreme Novices' Hurdle*, he was overtaken at the last hurdle by the 15/8 favourite, *My Tent Or Yours*, only to rally gamely on the run in to beat the market leader by half a length. ***Champagne Fever*** just missed out on a hat-trick of Cheltenham Festival victories in the 2014 *Racing Post Arkle Challenge Trophy Chase*. Having led all the way in the race, the 11/4 favourite was eventually beaten by a head in the dying strides, by the strong finishing 33/1 outsider, *Western Warhorse*.

In last year's Guide, I was a little concerned that **Stowaway** may turn out to be a stallion that produced a Cheltenham "one-hit wonder", as the impressive statistics, albeit from very few festival runs, was dominated by the now retired ***Champagne Fever***. But the 2017 festival performances from ***Champagne Classic***, ***Runfordave*** and ***The Worlds End*** in addition to ***Hidden Cyclone***'s 2nd place finish in the 2014 *Ryanair Chase*, has eliminated my doubts. In all likelihood, **Stowaway** will be represented by another record number of entries at the 2018 Cheltenham Festival and I would advise punters to pay serious attention to them.

Turgeon (USA)

Quote from the 2017 Cheltenham Festival Stallion Guide - "The speciality of **Turgeon** sired runners is encouraging runs in chase events without actually winning, as evidenced by the past decade's 16 from 18 top eight finishes."

Turgeon (32-y-o)								
Race Format	Miles	Won	Placed	Unplaced	Total	Win %	Place %
Hurdles	About 2m	0	0	2	2	0%	0%
	About 2m 4f	0	0	2	2	0%	0%
	About 3m	0	0	1	1	0%	0%
Chases	About 2m	0	0	0	0	-	-
	About 2m 4f	1	2	1	4	25%	75%
	About 3m	0	4	8	12	0%	33%
	About 4m	0	0	0	0	-	-
Bumper	About 2m	0	0	1	1	0%	0%
Total	**2008-2017**	**1**	**6**	**15**	**22**	**5%**	**32%**

At 32 years old, **Turgeon** is the oldest living stallion to appear in the 2018 Cheltenham Festival Stallion Guide and his two representatives at the 2017 Cheltenham Festival failed to make the old horse happy as neither of them completed their races. ***La Vaticane*** (50/1) was pulled up before the last in the *Fulke Walwyn Kim Muir Challenge Cup Amateur Riders' Handicap Chase* and ***Turcagua*** (66/1) was also pulled up when competing in the *Albert Bartlett Novices' Hurdle*.

In total, 13 of his offspring have registered 33 festival appearances, 22 of which have taken place within the past decade. Within these 33 runs, the progeny have competed in 9 hurdle events and 24 chases. All seven place positions and the single festival victory have been achieved over the Cheltenham fences. The highest finishing position that a **Turgeon** sired representative has recorded in a festival hurdle race is the 6th position claimed by ***Turko*** in the 2006 JCB Triumph Hurdle.

Of the 13 of **Turgeon**'s stock to have participated at a festival, six of them have experienced the roar of the festival crowds on at least three or more occasions and are responsible for 24 out of the total of 33 appearances. There are some familiar names amongst the six horses in question; ***Chapoturgeon*** (a 1st and 2nd from 6 runs); ***Exotic Dancer*** (a 2nd and 3rd from 4 runs); ***Turko*** (a 3rd from 4 runs); ***Turthen*** (a 2nd from 4 runs); ***Ma Filleule*** (twice a runner-up in 3 runs); and finally ***Turgeonev*** who in 3 appearances is the only one of the six to have raced on 3 or more occasions at the festival without picking up at least a place dividend.

The first of those mentioned above, ***Chapoturgeon***, stands alone as the only one of **Turgeon**'s progeny to have won a Cheltenham Festival race, when he was successful in the 2009 *Jewson Novices' Handicap Chase*, winning easily by 9 lengths. When it comes to **Turgeon**'s stock, ***Chapoturgeon*** holds three other 'firsts'. He was the first **Turgeon** bred runner to be pulled up whilst contesting a festival chase event, this being the 2013 *CGA Foxhunter Chase Challenge Cup*. In 2016, he became the oldest of all of **Turgeon**'s progeny to compete in a festival race, when at 12 years old, he lined up in the *St. James's Place Foxhunter Chase Challenge Cup*. And in that same race, he became the very first of **Turgeon**'s offspring to be parted from his rider, when he fell in the race two fences from home.

The highest rated of all **Turgeon**'s stock was ***Exotic Dancer*** who achieved two place positions in the 2007 and 2009 *totesport Cheltenham Gold Cup Chase*, both of which were won by the renowned *Kauto Star*. For a horse that raced three times in a Cheltenham Gold Cup and amassed a total of £800,000 in prize money, it is amazing to think that when ***Exotic Dancer*** finished 7th in his first festival appearance in the 2005 *Ladbrokes World Hurdle*, his odds were 150/1! Sadly, ***Exotic Dancer*** died of a heart attack after finishing 2nd in the *totesport Bowl Chase* at *Aintree* less than a month after his 3rd placing in the 2009 *Cheltenham Gold Cup*. He was just 9 years old.

Punters may be interested by the realisation that no **Turgeon** sired festival runner has ever finished higher than 6th on their festival debut, including the five of the progeny that have rewarded punters with a pay-out, their debut placings being ***Chapoturgeon*** 9th; ***Exotic Dancer*** 7th; ***Ma Filleule*** 13th; ***Turthen*** 7th; and ***Turko*** 6th. Of these five, ***Exotic Dancer***, ***Ma Filleule*** and ***Turthen*** all finished runner-up on their second festival appearances and ***Chapoturgeon*** went one better, securing a victory. ***Turko*** achieved his one placing from 4 festival races on his third outing, when he finished 3rd in the 2008 *Ryanair Chase*.

In summary, with a best placing of 6th in nine attempts over the smaller obstacles, we can forget about **Turgeon**'s progeny when it comes to the festival's hurdle races. And I'm also inclined to disregard the offspring that are making their festival debuts as no **Turgeon** bred festival debutant has ever finished higher than 6th. Therefore, if there is any chance of a **Turgeon** sired representative providing punters with a pay-out, the runner needs to satisfy two criteria. First, the horse needs to hold an entry in a festival chase of around 2½m or 3m, these being the only two race categories within which **Turgeon**'s offspring have registered top three finishes; and secondly, the selection should already have experience of at least one Cheltenham Festival outing. All of which, should they turn up and be entered in an applicable race, points us towards the two runners that were pulled up at last year's festival, ***La Vaticane*** and ***Turcagua***, neither of which appear attractive betting propositions.

As far as this old stallion goes, I recommend we give 2018 a miss and see what **Turgeon** brings to the festival party in 2019.

Vinnie Roe (IRE)

Vinnie Roe was not featured in the 2017 Cheltenham Festival Stallion Guide.

Vinnie Roe (20-y-o)							
Race Format	*Miles*	*Won*	*Placed*	*Unplaced*	*Total*	*Win %*	*Place %*
Hurdles	About 2m	0	0	2	2	0%	0%
	About 2m 4f	0	1	3	4	0%	25%
	About 3m	0	1	3	4	0%	25%
Chases	About 2m	0	1	1	2	0%	50%
	About 2m 4f	0	0	0	0	-	-
	About 3m	0	0	1	1	0%	0%
	About 4m	0	0	3	3	0%	0%
Bumper	About 2m	0	0	1	1	0%	0%
Total	**2008-2017**	**0**	**3**	**14**	**17**	**0%**	**18%**

Considering that there had only been nine of **Vinnie Roe**'s stock represented at Cheltenham Festivals between 2013 and 2016, the progeny were somewhat mob-handed in 2017 as eight **Vinnie Roe** bred horses were entered in seven of the festival's 28 races. With just seventeen festival runs to consider, it is early days and so any trends analysis needs to be considered with a great deal of caution. Nevertheless, the early signals suggest that those towards the fore of the betting market are performing reasonably well and it will be interesting to see if this pattern continues at the 2018 Cheltenham Festival and beyond.

Although the progeny are yet to win a festival race, the *Harry Fry* trained ***Neon Wolf***, came almighty close to registering a victory at last year's meeting when he finished runner-up to *Willoughby Court* in the *Neptune Investment Management Novices' Hurdle*. ***Neon Wolf***, who was unbeaten and the warm 2/1 favourite, almost ran a perfect race. He jumped fluently throughout until he came to the very last hurdle where he landed awkwardly and stumbled, which probably cost him the race. He rallied gamely up the hill but didn't quite get up to beat the game front running *Willoughby Court* who prevailed by a head to claim victory. Unfortunately, in August 2017, the rising star of *Harry Fry*'s yard suffered a freak accident resulting in a severe tendon injury. ***Neon Wolf*** could not be saved, a devastating blow to his connections.

In the 2017 *Pertemps Network Final Handicap Hurdle*, the **Vinnie Roe** sired ***Barney Dwan*** registered another runner-up finish for the offspring, when losing out to the progressive *Presenting Percy*. Trained by *Fergal O'Brien* and ridden by *Paddy Brennan*, it could be said that ***Barney Dwan*** had been rather unlucky in three of his previous four races. He finished 2nd having blundered at the last when 3 lengths ahead at *Kempton* in November 2016; was brought down three out when travelling well at *Wincanton* a month later; and in January 2017, he was disputing a close second when unseating his rider at *Warwick*. He wasn't unlucky here though, putting in an excellent effort but beaten fair and square by *Presenting Percy* who stayed on very strongly after the last to go clear and win by 3¾ lengths.

The one other place dividend recorded by **Vinnie Roe**'s progeny occurred at the 2014 Cheltenham Festival in the last race of the meeting, the *Johnny Henderson Grand Annual Chase Challenge Cup*

Handicap, where the *Emma Lavelle* trained ***Claret Cloak*** who was one of the joint 6/1 favourites finished third.

In the opening paragraph, I highlighted that **Vinnie Roe** sired runners, towards the front of the market, have performed reasonably well at festival meetings and ***Neon Wolf***, ***Barney Dwan*** and ***Claret Cloak***, who were all placed, represent three of the eight of **Vinnie Roe**'s stock that returned odds of less than 20/1. Of the other five, ***Royal Caviar*** (6/1) finished 4th in last year's *Racing Post Arkle Challenge Trophy Novices' Chase*; ***Our Vinnie*** (7/1) was brought down at half-way in the 2013 *Albert Bartlett Novices' Hurdle*; and the other three performed poorly. Punters are advised to forget about supporting **Vinnie Roe** bred outsiders. Of the nine festival runners who lined up at odds of 20/1 or greater, two finished 9th, five were pulled up and the other two were placed 16th and 18th.

With just seventeen festival runs to go on, there is nowhere near enough data on which to make foolhardy conclusions, but on the basis that 50% of **Vinnie Roe** sired runners that had an SP of less than 20/1, delivered a top 4 finish, an each-way bet on those towards the front of the market may well produce a pay-out. As for the outsiders, ignore them.

Voix Du Nord (FR)

Quote from the 2017 Cheltenham Festival Stallion Guide - "If one had placed a £1.00 each-way bet on all 18 festival runs of **Voix Du Nord**'s offspring, the outcome would have been a loss of £15.10. Despite this, in looking at the overall record of the progeny, I think a profit for punters is just around the corner."

Voix Du Nord (Died as a 12-y-o in 2013)							
Race Format	*Miles*	*Won*	*Placed*	*Unplaced*	*Total*	*Win %*	*Place %*
Hurdles	About 2m	1	1	4	6	17%	33%
	About 2m 4f	1	2	3	6	17%	50%
	About 3m	0	1	2	3	0%	33%
Chases	About 2m	0	0	2	2	0%	0%
	About 2m 4f	1	0	8	9	11%	11%
	About 3m	0	0	0	0	-	-
	About 4m	0	0	0	0	-	-
Bumper	About 2m	0	0	0	0	-	-
Total	**2008-2017**	**3**	**4**	**19**	**26**	**12%**	**27%**

If we take the fifteen of **Voix Du Nord**'s progeny that have appeared at the Cheltenham Festival, making up the total of 26 runs, three of them have won and a further two have been placed, which equates to a satisfying one third of the offspring registering at least a festival placing. The three festival wins as shown in the table above represents a 12% win strike rate which is better than the majority of stallions featured in this Guide, and the win and place hit rate is a reassuring 27%.

The majority of **Voix Du Nord** bred festival runs have taken place at the last two meetings, with the progeny securing two wins and two places from 15 appearances, and there is no reason why further success from this stallion won't continue as we approach the 2018 Cheltenham Festival. The dilemma for punters is that despite the positive results, it has been frustratingly difficult to make profits when backing the offspring. Indeed, 2014 is the sole year in which one would have made a profit in backing all of **Voix Du Nord**'s festival representatives blind to level stakes. With the earliest figure being 2015, to a £1.00 each-way stake, the last three festival meetings would have produced losses of £5.50, £11.20 and £5.45. To date, inclusive of the first and only appearance from **Voix Du Nord**'s stock in 2013, (***Taquin Du Seuil***'s 6th place in the *Neptune Investment Management Novices' Hurdle*), supporting all 26 of **Voix Du Nord**'s festival runners to a £1.00 each-way stake, calculates into a loss of £20.55.

Of course, the above losses are down to the offspring's three winners and four placings being towards the front of the betting market and therefore coming in at relatively short odds, but I am far from convinced that this is a trend that will continue. For one thing, the majority of **Voix du Nord**'s runners have finished in their festival races nearer the front than towards the back. 17 of the 26 festival runs have resulted in the runner finishing in the first 8 positions and four of the appearances resulted in the **Voix Du Nord** sired entry falling or unseating the jockey. In my view, had the four in question managed to complete the course, one would have won its race at a price of 14/1, and two of the other three would have secured a top six finish. The remaining 5 of the 26 runners finished outside the front ten.

The unluckiest year for **Voix Du Nord**'s progeny was at the 2016 Cheltenham Festival where of the seven runners who set out in their respective races, only three of them managed to complete the course. Freakishly, all four occasions in which horse and jockey have parted company occurred at the 2016 meeting, the offspring completing their races in all of their other 22 festival appearances. Of the four fallers, although one can rarely be certain as to the likely outcome of a contest had a horse not fallen, having watched the race replay on a number of occasions, my view is that ***Voix Du Reve*** would have prevailed and won the 2016 *Fred Winter Juvenile Handicap Hurdle*. The **Voix Du Nord** sired 14/1 chance was making headway three from home, travelling well and mounting a strong challenge when falling at the last. Had ***Voix Du Reve*** stayed on his feet (and bear in mind he would have been assisted in the run to the line by the hugely experienced jockey *Ruby Walsh*) and won, then the £20.55 loss of backing all 26 of **Voix Du Nord**'s festival entries would have been pretty much eliminated. But the horse fell and did not win and it is the printed result that matters. The Cheltenham Festival is awash with stories like this with punters consoling themselves that their selection was unlucky.

Of the eight **Voix Du Nord** bred entries at the 2017 Cheltenham Festival, the best performance was saved for Friday's opening race, where the *Philip Hobbs* trained 5/2 favourite, ***Defi Du Seuil*** was highly impressive when running on strongly to land the *JCB Triumph Hurdle* by 5 lengths. ***Defi Du Seuil*** is entered for the *Unibet Champion Hurdle Challenge Trophy* at this year's festival and if he runs, it will be interesting to see how he prospers following what was a very disappointing effort in his first race of this season at *Ascot* in November. In the *Coral Hurdle (registered as the Ascot Hurdle)*, the 10/11 favourite was struggling in the home straight, and finished 4th out of the five runners, leaving *Philip Hobbs* baffled by the poor performance. After the race, ***Defi Du Seuil*** was pushed out to 16/1 in the *Champion Hurdle* betting.

On the opening day of last year's meeting, ***Vroum Vroum Mag*** was attempting to follow up her facile victory of the previous year in the *OLBG Mares' Hurdle*, but 2017 provided the strongest edition of this race to date, with two other top class mares to race against. *Ruby Walsh* who rode ***Vroum Vroum Mag*** to victory in 2016 at 4/6 odds on, abandoned the mare in 2017 in favour of the other contender from *Willie Mullins*' yard, *Limini*, who lined up as the 6/4 favourite for the race. As it turned out, both horses were beaten by the *Gordon Elliott* trained *Apple's Jade* (7/2), who rallied gamely on the run-in to beat ***Vroum Vroum Mag*** (11/4) by 1½ lengths, with *Limini* a nose back in third. The following day, the 10 year old, ***Taquin Du Seuil*** was enjoying what was his fifth festival appearance. Not only was ***Taquin Du Seuil*** the very first of **Voix Du Nord**'s offspring to line up in a festival race as highlighted earlier, but he was also the stallion's first festival winner when he landed the *JLT Novices' Chase* in 2014. For the next two years, ***Taquin Du Seuil*** finished unplaced in two attempts in the *Ryanair Chase*, so at the 2017 Cheltenham Festival, trainer *Jonjo O'Neill* decided to run him over hurdles, where the 12/1 chance put in a super effort to finish runner-up to *Supasundae* in the *Coral Cup Handicap Hurdle*.

I'm quite surprised that **Voix Du Nord**'s offspring have only managed one top three finish in the festival's chase events, this being ***Taquin Du Seuil***'s victory in the *JLT Novices' Chase*. Perhaps the progeny are better suited to hurdles but only more festival runs over the bigger obstacles will confirm whether or not this is the case. To date, the results are definitely better over hurdles with a 40% win and place strike rate compared to just 9% over fences. Further analysis reveals that the two wins and four places achieved all came from the eight **Voix Du Nord** sired runners who went off at odds of 14/1 or shorter. The two who failed to hit a top three finish have already been mentioned; ***Taquin Du Seuil***'s 6th in the 2013 *Neptune Investment Management Novices' Hurdle* and ***Voix Du Reve*** falling at the last hurdle when looking likely to win in the 2016 *Fred Winter Juvenile Handicap Hurdle*. If one had placed a £1.00 each-way bet on all eight of **Voix Du Nord**'s offspring who lined up at odds of 14/1 or shorter in the festival's hurdle races, the outcome would be a profit of £5.05. For the record, the seven 'outsiders' who raced at odds of 16/1 or greater, weren't too far off the pace. Five of them recorded finishing positions of between 5th and 8th in their races, and in the 2016 *Albert Bartlett Novices' Hurdle*, the 28/1 chance, ***Bachasson***, was in the process of running a respectable race, disputing 5th and about six lengths off the pace, before he blundered and unseated his jockey at the last.

As we approach the 2018 Cheltenham Festival, although I would not dissuade anyone from placing a bet on a **Voix Du Nord** sired entry in the chase events, at this juncture, the safest recommendation is to support the progeny's runners in the festival's hurdle races; and especially if they are towards the fore of the market at 14/1 or less.

Westerner (GB)

Quote from the 2017 Cheltenham Festival Stallion Guide - "Of even more significance is the huge profit to be gained in backing the stallion's festival entries, which stands at a mammoth £65.00 if one had placed a £1.00 win bet on all 30 of **Westerner** sired festival runners to date."

Westerner (19-y-o)								
Race Format	*Miles*	*Won*	*Placed*	*Unplaced*	*Total*	*Win %*	*Place %*
Hurdles	About 2m	0	1	2	3	0%	33%
	About 2m 4f	0	1	7	8	0%	13%
	About 3m	1	1	11	13	8%	15%
Chases	About 2m	2	0	2	4	50%	50%
	About 2m 4f	1	0	5	6	17%	17%
	About 3m	0	0	5	5	0%	0%
	About 4m	0	0	1	1	0%	0%
Bumper	About 2m	0	0	4	4	0%	0%
Total	**2008-2017**	**4**	**3**	**37**	**44**	**9%**	**16%**

Marking the 40th anniversary of her accession in London's Guildhall on 24th November 1992, *Queen Elizabeth II* brought the Latin phrase "annus horribilis" to prominence when she said, "1992 is not a year on which I shall look back with undiluted pleasure. In the words of one of my more sympathetic correspondents, it has turned out to be an annus horribilis". The phrase, meaning "horrible year", is a very apt description for how supporters of **Westerner**'s offspring will remember the 2017 Cheltenham Festival. The stallion was represented on 14 occasions last season and every single wager on a **Westerner** bred runner turned out to be a loser.

Historically, supporters of **Westerner**'s offspring had been spoilt with sizable profits, indeed a profit of £71.65 to a £1.00 each-way stake if backing blind all 30 of the progeny's previous festival runners. In those 30 festival appearances, **Westerner**'s stock had amassed four victories and three place dividends, at rewarding odds of between 9/1 and 33/1. In comparison, at last year's Cheltenham Festival, 9 of the 14 **Westerner** bred runners lined up at between these same prices of 9/1 and 33/1, and only one of them managed to finish in the top six places, courtesy of ***Cole Harden***'s 4th place finish, at odds of 9/1, in the *Sun Bets Stayer's Hurdle*. Of the other five appearances from the progeny, the three 66/1 outsiders finished down the field, but the two shortest priced horses, ***Empire Of Dirt*** and ***Western Ryder***, performed respectfully. The *Gordon Elliott* trained ***Empire Of Dirt*** (11/4), who won the *Brown Advisory & Merriebelle Stable Plate* at the 2016 Cheltenham Festival, missed out on a place dividend when finishing 4th in the *Ryanair Chase*. And at odds of 7/1, ***Western Ryder*** put in a strong finish to claim 5th position in the *Weatherbys Champion Bumper*, less than 3½ lengths behind impressive winner, *Fayonagh*.

Because of the dismal 2017 festival results, the win and win/place strike rates of **Westerner**'s offspring have deteriorated appreciably. Even so, due to the prices returned for the seven **Westerner** bred runners who won or were placed, supporting the progeny blind to level stakes would still have delivered a sizable profitable return of £43.65 to a £1.00 each-way stake. Of the four festival winners, the shortest priced of them is ***Cole Harden***, who was victorious in the 2015 *Ladbrokes World Hurdle* at odds of 14/1. It was a well-deserved and first ever Cheltenham Festival victory for both the trainer, *Warren Greatrex*, and jockey, *Gavin Sheehan*. At the preceding year's festival in the 2014 *Arkle*, ***Western Warhorse*** (33/1) sprang a major surprise when he managed to get up on the line to beat the *Willie Mullins* trained favourite *Champagne Fever* by a head. The last time that the *Arkle* winner was returned at double digit odds was when *Flagship Uberalles* won the 1999 renewal at odds of 11/1. **Westerner**'s progeny recorded a second 2m chase victory in the final festival race of the 2016 Cheltenham Festival, the *Johnny Henderson Grand Annual Chase Challenge Cup*, when ***Solar Impulse*** (28/1), ridden by *Sam Twiston-Davies*, ran on strongly to beat *Dandridge* by 3¾ lengths. And the fourth victory for the stock, courtesy of ***Empire Of Dirt***'s 16/1 success in the 2016 *Brown Advisory & Merriebelle Stable Plate*, has already been touched upon above. Ridden by *Bryan Cooper*, ***Empire Of Dirt*** was well in command after leading two out, and won the race comfortably.

I guess we are all pondering as to whether last year was genuinely a one-off "annus horribilis" for **Westerner**'s progeny or conceivably the start of a trend of dismal festival results. Due to the significant profit harvested previously, my hunch is that punters should still be very interested in this stallion's festival entries, and adjudge that for **Westerner**'s representatives at Cheltenham 2017, it was simply a "bad four days at the office".

Winged Love (IRE)

Quote from the 2017 Cheltenham Festival Stallion Guide - "When it comes to **Winged Love**'s stock, here is the rule for punters. Should a horse sired by **Winged Love** win or be placed at a Cheltenham Festival for the first time in its career, place a very large each-way bet on the same horse the next time that it appears in a festival race! Admittedly this is a peculiar coincidence, but the truth is that when ***Bostons Angel***, ***Hunt Ball***, ***Josses Hill*** and now ***Bless The Wings*** all managed to win or be placed in a festival race, the very next time they lined up in a Cheltenham Festival contest, all four of them gained a place dividend."

Winged Love (Died as a 23-y-o in 2015)							
Race Format	*Miles*	***Won***	***Placed***	***Unplaced***	***Total***	***Win %***	***Place %***
Hurdles	About 2m	0	1	3	4	0%	25%
	About 2m 4f	0	0	0	0	-	-
	About 3m	0	0	5	5	0%	0%
Chases	About 2m	0	1	4	5	0%	20%
	About 2m 4f	1	1	9	11	9%	18%
	About 3m	1	1	8	10	10%	20%
	About 4m	0	3	5	8	0%	38%
Bumper	About 2m	0	0	1	1	0%	0%
Total	**2008-2017**	**2**	**7**	**35**	**44**	**5%**	**20%**

Back in 2004, the very first of **Winged Love**'s offspring made an appearance at the Cheltenham Festival, when the *Jonjo O'Neill* trained ***Cherub***, just missed out on a place by finishing 4th at odds of 16/1, in the *JCB Triumph Hurdle*. Since then, 23 more of the progeny have tacked a further 47 festival races, of which 44 have taken place in the past decade. All of the festival wins and places have been achieved by just 4 of the **Winged Love**'s stock, and all four of them have managed to record a win or place more than once.

Bizarrely, the highest rated chaser by some distance to be bred by **Winged Love**, failed to even place at a Cheltenham Festival, despite trying on four occasions. The ill-fated ***Twist Magic***, trained by *Paul Nicholls*, was only eight years old when, in December 2010, he suffered a fatal fall two from home when leading in the Grade 2 *Peterborough Chase* at *Newbury*. Nine months earlier, he was running for the third time in a row in the *Seasons Holidays Queen Mother Champion Chase* at the Cheltenham Festival when having blundered four out, he was pulled up. Undoubtedly his best race at the Cheltenham Festival was his first when as a five year old in the 2007 *Irish Independent Arkle Challenge Trophy Chase*, he was running a great race, staying on and just a length down in third place when he fell two fences from home. The next three runs were all in the aforementioned *Queen Mother Champion Chase* when he failed to sparkle on all three occasions between 2008 and 2010. With accumulated earnings of £579,969 and a best ever official rating of 175, it is surprising that ***Twist Magic*** disappointed when it came to competing at Cheltenham's biggest event, especially considering that of the next five highest rated chasers sired by **Winged Love**, four of them have tasted festival success, and on more than one occasion.

Hunt Ball, who managed to attain an official rating of 162 in April 2013, rose through the handicap ranks at amazing speed between November 2011 and February 2012. In just four months, the horse won six races and climbed from a mark of 69 to 142, before being raised another 12 pounds as a result of his Cheltenham Festival victory in the listed 2012 *Pulteney Land Investments Novices' Handicap* over 2½ miles. The following season, ***Hunt Ball***'s trainer, *Kieran Burke*, entered him in the Grade 3 *Byrne Group Plate*, and the horse secured a fourth place dividend in yet another satisfying run. Interestingly, two months later, ***Hunt Ball***'s owner *Anthony Knott*, sold the gelding to *Atlantic Equine*. The American-based syndicate's intention was to achieve success for the horse in America, but after four inauspicious runs of finishing nearer last than first, the new owners decided to send him back to the UK. Now trained by *Nicky Henderson,* in the horse's third Cheltenham Festival race, the 2014 *Ryanair Chase*, ***Hunt Ball*** finished fourth and just outside the places. In 2015, and now ten years of age, in his 4th and final festival appearance, he finished well down the field in the *Brown Advisory & Merriebelle Stable Plate.*

Rated 10lbs below ***Hunt Ball***, off a highest mark of 152, can be found the only other **Winged Love** bred Cheltenham Festival winner, the *Jessica Harrington* trained, ***Bostons Angel***, who off a mark of 146, landed the *RSA Chase* in 2011 at odds of 16/1. Raised 6lbs after this success, ***Bostons Angel*** was never quite the same horse afterwards, missed the 2012 Cheltenham Festival, and failed to register a win in any of his last 14 outings. However, in the midst of this winless streak, he did manage to run another sound race on his last festival appearance, when finishing 4th and picking up a place dividend in the 2013 *Glenfarclas Handicap Chase*.

At last year's festival meeting, five of **Winged Love**'s progeny lined up at Cheltenham, of which two, ***Joey Sasa*** and ***Rock Gone***, were making their festival debuts; both finished outside the first six in their respective races. ***Some Plan*** was back at the festival for the third season running, but once again, this time in the *Racing Post Arkle Challenge Trophy Novices' Chase*, he finished nearer last than first. ***Josses Hill*** was running in his fourth Cheltenham Festival and making his second appearance in the *Ryanair Chase*. In the 2016 renewal, he finished half-way down the field in 8th place having been outpaced and weakening up the hill. It was a similar story last year when off his highest official rating of 158, he finished 5th of eight runners, again being outpaced and weakening when it mattered. The *Nicky Henderson* trained, ***Josses Hill***, had enjoyed better fortune in his first two festival appearances over the minimum distance of two miles. In his first festival appearance, at 14/1, he finished runner-up to *Vautour* in the *Sky Bet Supreme Novices' Hurdle*. The following season, this time over the larger obstacles in the *Racing Post Arkle Challenge Trophy Chase*, ***Josses Hill*** did not disappoint backers when staying on to finish in third, returning a price of 12/1.

Like ***Josses Hill***, there are a reasonable number of horses that have managed to stay injury free to turn up at four consecutive festival appearances, but I think it is a tiny minority that have appeared at six consecutive Cheltenham Festivals, like the *Gordon Elliott* trained ***Bless The Wings***, whose highest Official rating is 154. Previously at *Alan King*'s yard at *Barbury Castle*, ***Bless The Wings*** was rather disappointing in all three of his appearances between 2012 and 2014, finishing down the field on every occasion. Having moved to *Gordon Elliott*'s stable in the summer of 2014, now ten years of age and at a price of 28/1, ***Bless The Wings*** wasn't particularly fancied to trouble the leaders when he lined up in the 2015 *Fulke Walwyn Kim Muir Challenge Cup Handicap Chase.* However, the change of scenery had clearly had an effect, as *Nina Carberry* rode ***Bless The Wings*** into the runner-up spot. At the 2016 Cheltenham Festival, ***Bless The Wings*** was entered in the cross country *Glenfarclas Chase*. The horse had already raced over course and distance in the November and December of 2015, where both races had been won by the *Enda Bolger* trained, *Josies Orders*. ***Bless The Wings*** finished third and 6 lengths behind the winner in November, and fourth and more than 25 lengths behind the same horse a month later. When it came to the festival race, once again ***Bless The Wings*** was unfancied, despite being ridden by the excellent amateur jockey, *Jamie Codd*. As it turned out, the result was not too different to what had happened over course and distance twice previously, although this time ***Bless The Wings***, at 33/1, managed to finish just 1¼ lengths away from the favourite, *Josies Orders*. On the day, both horses finished 2nd and 3rd, behind the *Aidan Coleman* ridden, *Any Currency*. Five months later, however, *Any Currency* was disqualified due to a positive post-race drugs test, thereby *Josies Orders* being promoted to first and ***Bless The Wings*** to second. At last year's festival, ***Bless The Wings*** finished runner-up in the *Glenfarclas Chase* for the second year running, finishing some 9 lengths behind his strong finishing stablemate *Cause Of Causes*, who was enjoying his 3rd victory at the festival in his fifth festival appearance. Runner-up, then, for three successive years, ***Bless the Wings*** clearly loves Cheltenham, and for the first time since he joined Gordon Elliott's yard in 2014, he claimed his first win at the course on 15th December 2017, at Cheltenham's International Meeting, where he beat off the two *Enda Bolger* trained runners, *Cantlow* and *Josies Orders*, to win the *Glenfarclas Cross Country Handicap Chase* at a price of 12/1. It will be some feat if *Gordon Elliott* can get ***Bless The Wings*** to Cheltenham this spring for a seventh consecutive appearance at the festival. And should he be entered again in the *Glenfarclas Cross Country Steeple Chase*, can he once again secure a place dividend, or even perhaps win? It will be a fantastic achievement especially considering the horse is now thirteen years old. Connections should take encouragement from the 2016 renewal of the race, where the first past the post before being disqualified some five months later, was the *Martin Keighley* trained ***Any Currency***; a 13 year old.

With regard to recommendations for the 2018 Cheltenham Festival, it is interesting to note that the four horses sired by **Winged Love** that have tasted festival success have all registered a top official rating of between 152 and 162. Based upon this, I believe it is unlikely that any of this stallion's offspring will trouble the judge at Cheltenham unless they are currently rated above the mid-140s. All of which points the finger at just three horses sired by **Winged Love** who have the potential to win or be placed at this year's meeting. The three horses in question are triple festival runner-up ***Bless The Wings*** (as highlighted above), who won December's *Glenfarclas Cross Country Handicap Chase* off a mark of 147; ***Josses Hill***, currently on a mark of 150, and whose most recent race was in December 2017, when finishing second behind *Top Notch* in the Grade 2 *Peterborough Chase* at *Taunton*; and finally, ***Perfect Candidate***, whose last appearance was when winning the *BetVictor.com Handicap Chase* at Cheltenham's November Meeting, off an Official Rating of 152. The victory reads well, but there are two obvious negatives against ***Perfect Candidate*** in that he is a veteran chaser of eleven years old and in his two previous festival races, he has finished well down the field on both occasions.

Index Table by Stallion

This table shows the British Horseracing Association (BHA) and Irish Horseracing Regulatory Board (I.H.R.B) Official Ratings (as of January 2018) for National Hunt horses. Only horses that were showing an official rating of 130 or greater in January 2018 are listed. Index is in alphabetical order and only for stallions listed within this Guide. In order to distinguish between BHA and I.H.R.B Official Ratings, the I.H.R.B entries are shown in *italics*.

				Official Ratings as of Jan 2018	
Sire	*Horse*	*Age*	*Sex*	*Hurdles*	*Chase*
Al Namix	Abricot De L'Oasis	8	g	130	132
Al Namix	Ballyhill	7	g		138
Al Namix	Dear Sire	6	g	137	
Al Namix	Mr Mix	7	g		144
Al Namix	Saphir Du Rheu	9	g		160
Al Namix	Space Oddity	7	g		138
Astarabad	Traffic Fluide	8	g		151
Astarabad	Whisper	10	g		167
Authorized	Altruism	8	g	140	135
Authorized	*Automated*	*7*	*g*	*138*	
Authorized	Boite	8	g	148	
Authorized	Ennistown	8	g	135	
Authorized	Peak To Peak	6	g	130	
Authorized	Sir Chauvelin	6	g	133	
Authorized	Sternrubin	7	g		143
Authorized	*Tiger Roll*	*8*	*g*	*140*	*151*
Authorized	Totalize	9	g		141
Authorized	Zamdy Man	9	g		137
Authorized	Zubayr	6	g	135	
Ballingarry	Ahead Of The Curve	6	g	137	
Ballingarry	Aubusson	9	g	141	135
Ballingarry	Ballywood	4	g	135	
Ballingarry	Diego Du Charmil	6	g		143
Ballingarry	Katgary	8	g	136	135
Ballingarry	Kauto Riko	7	g		130
Beneficial	*A Genie In Abottle*	*7*	*g*		*149*
Beneficial	Ballinvarrig	11	g		132
Beneficial	Ballyben	10	g	123	133
Beneficial	*Ben Dundee*	*6*	*g*	*134*	
Beneficial	Benatar	6	g		149
Beneficial	Benbens	13	g		138
Beneficial	Bentelimar	9	g		136
Beneficial	*Bonny Kate*	*8*	*m*		*138*
Beneficial	Brandon Hill	10	g		133
Beneficial	Classic Ben	5	g	130	
Beneficial	*Colms Dream*	*9*	*g*	*116*	*140*
Beneficial	*De Plotting Shed*	*8*	*g*		*143*
Beneficial	Eastlake	12	g		147
Beneficial	Forever Field	8	g	134	134
Beneficial	*Forge Meadow*	*6*	*m*	*142*	

				Official Ratings as of Jan 2018	
Sire	Horse	Age	Sex	Hurdles	Chase
Beneficial	*Hurricane Ben*	*9*	*g*		*145*
Beneficial	*Jetstream Jack*	*8*	*g*	*137*	*140*
Beneficial	Kilcrea Vale	8	g		137
Beneficial	Knocknanuss	8	g	135	
Beneficial	Lady Buttons	8	m	134	138
Beneficial	*Livelovelaugh*	*8*	*g*		*137*
Beneficial	*Mala Beach*	*10*	*g*		*156*
Beneficial	Maria's Benefit	6	m	149	
Beneficial	*Marlbrook*	*10*	*g*	*128*	*137*
Beneficial	*Monksland*	*11*	*g*	*145*	*143*
Beneficial	More Of That	10	g		151
Beneficial	Mr Whipped	5	g	146	
Beneficial	Pawn Star	8	g		132
Beneficial	*Realt Mor*	*13*	*g*	*123*	*134*
Beneficial	*Red Devil Lads*	*9*	*g*	*132*	*130*
Beneficial	Red River	5	g	137	
Beneficial	Scotchtown	6	g		133
Beneficial	Sego Success	10	g		134
Beneficial	Top Ville Ben	6	g	142	
Beneficial	Upswing	10	g		139
Califet	Adrien Du Pont	6	g		145
Califet	*Bamako Moriviere*	*7*	*g*		*150*
Califet	Brahms De Clermont	7	g	135	
Califet	Calipto	8	g		131
Califet	*Cilaos Emery*	*6*	*g*	*153*	
Califet	*Clarcam*	*8*	*g*		*151*
Califet	Don Bersy	5	g	133	
Cape Cross	Leoncavallo	6	g	133	
Cape Cross	*Wakea*	*7*	*g*	*146*	
Cape Cross	Waterlord	7	g	135	
Definite Article	Definite Future	9	g		136
Definite Article	Definitly Red	9	g		167
Definite Article	*Mountain King*	*9*	*g*		*134*
Definite Article	Pingshou	8	g	148	
Definite Article	Sizing Platinum	10	g	135	148
Dom Alco	Antartica De Thaix	8	m		141
Dom Alco	Brio Conti	7	g	145	145
Dom Alco	Vic De Touzaine	9	g		139
Dom Alco	Vicente	9	g		151
Dom Alco	Vivaldi Collonges	9	g		135
Dr Massini	*Doctor Phoenix*	*10*	*g*		*155*
Dr Massini	Forgotten Gold	12	g		141
Dr Massini	Foxtail Hill	9	g		143
Dr Massini	*Massini's Trap*	*9*	*g*	*132*	
Dr Massini	Mr Medic	7	g		134
Dr Massini	Three Faces West	10	g		144
Flemensfirth	*A Rated*	*7*	*g*		*135*
Flemensfirth	Ainchea	5	g	139	
Flemensfirth	Aqua Dude	8	g		139
Flemensfirth	*Arctic Skipper*	*9*	*g*	*120*	*145*

				Official Ratings as of Jan 2018	
Sire	***Horse***	***Age***	***Sex***	***Hurdles***	***Chase***
Flemensfirth	Chooseyourweapon	5	g	134	
Flemensfirth	Closing Ceremony	9	g	135	
Flemensfirth	*Coney Island*	*7*	*g*		*162*
Flemensfirth	*Conrad Hastings*	*7*	*g*		*143*
Flemensfirth	Coole Hall	6	g	137	
Flemensfirth	Emperor's Choice	11	g		131
Flemensfirth	Firth Of The Clyde	13	g		140
Flemensfirth	Flemcara	6	g	139	
Flemensfirth	Full Irish	7	g		135
Flemensfirth	*Granny Biddy*	*7*	*m*	*135*	
Flemensfirth	Highland Lodge	12	g		135
Flemensfirth	*Invitation Only*	*7*	*g*		*153*
Flemensfirth	*Isleofhopendreams*	*11*	*g*	*130*	*135*
Flemensfirth	*Jett*	*7*	*g*		*142*
Flemensfirth	*Jetz*	*6*	*g*	*138*	
Flemensfirth	Knockgraffon	8	g		145
Flemensfirth	Lastbutnotleast	8	m	135	135
Flemensfirth	Lostintranslation	6	g	134	
Flemensfirth	Minella Daddy	8	g		137
Flemensfirth	Molly The Dolly	7	m	130	
Flemensfirth	Mosspark	10	g		130
Flemensfirth	*Noble Endeavor*	*9*	*g*		*154*
Flemensfirth	O O Seven	8	g		152
Flemensfirth	One Track Mind	8	g	153	153
Flemensfirth	Padge	9	g	132	
Flemensfirth	Poetic Rhythm	7	g	148	
Flemensfirth	*Prince Of Scars*	*8*	*g*	*150*	*139*
Flemensfirth	Red Rising	7	g	132	
Flemensfirth	Robinsfirth	9	g		148
Flemensfirth	*Rock On The Moor*	*10*	*m*		*135*
Flemensfirth	Shannon Bridge	5	g	142	
Flemensfirth	Sizing Codelco	9	g		154
Flemensfirth	*Space Cadet*	*8*	*g*		*132*
Flemensfirth	Strong Pursuit	8	g	139	139
Flemensfirth	*Sumos Novios*	*10*	*g*		*144*
Flemensfirth	The Last Samuri	10	g	156	159
Flemensfirth	Three Musketeers	8	g	138	146
Flemensfirth	Three Ways	7	g	135	135
Flemensfirth	Topofthegame	6	g	142	
Flemensfirth	Two Taffs	8	g		149
Flemensfirth	Viva Steve	10	g		138
Flemensfirth	Waiting Patiently	7	g		164
Galileo	*Boherbuoy*	*6*	*g*	*130*	
Galileo	*Heist*	*8*	*g*	*121*	*131*
Galileo	*Housesofparliament*	*5*	*g*	*131*	
Galileo	Shelford	9	g	140	129
Galileo	Stamp Your Feet	6	g	135	
Galileo	*Supasundae*	*8*	*g*	*159*	
Germany	*Faugheen*	*10*	*g*	*172*	
Germany	Germany Calling	9	g		139

Sire	Horse	Age	Sex	Official Ratings as of Jan 2018 Hurdles	Chase
Germany	*Samcro*	*6*	*g*	*153*	
Gold Well	Arctic Gold	7	g		132
Gold Well	Bally Longford	10	g		131
Gold Well	Ballyboker Breeze	10	g	130	
Gold Well	Better Getalong	7	g	138	
Gold Well	Chidswell	9	g		132
Gold Well	Clondaw Cian	8	g		131
Gold Well	Daklondike	6	g		139
Gold Well	Dark Flame	9	g		131
Gold Well	*General Principle*	*9*	*g*	*132*	*139*
Gold Well	*Goose Man*	*6*	*g*		*133*
Gold Well	*Kylecrue*	*11*	*g*	*133*	*137*
Gold Well	Looking Well	9	g		132
Gold Well	Mysteree	10	g		138
Gold Well	Ozzy Thomas	8	g		137
Gold Well	Poker School	8	g		132
Gold Well	Saints And Sinners	10	g		135
Gold Well	Shoal Bay	5	g	136	
Gold Well	*Sutton Manor*	*7*	*g*		*138*
Gold Well	The Unit	7	g	142	142
High Chaparral	Altior	8	g		170
High Chaparral	Different Gravey	8	g	140	140
High Chaparral	High Secret	7	g	137	
High Chaparral	*Landofhopeandglory*	*5*	*g*		*132*
High Chaparral	Thumb Stone Blues	8	g		131
Kalanisi	Barters Hill	8	g	142	
Kalanisi	Brain Power	7	g		157
Kalanisi	Kalashnikov	5	g	141	
Kalanisi	Templehills	7	g		136
Kapgarde	*Alisier D'Irlande*	*8*	*g*		*148*
Kapgarde	As De Mee	8	g		149
Kapgarde	Cap Soleil	5	m	136	
Kapgarde	Clan Des Obeaux	6	g		155
Kapgarde	Dieg Man	5	g	130	
Kapgarde	Dolos	5	g	135	144
Kapgarde	Fixe Le Kap	6	g	143	
Kapgarde	Garde La Victoire	9	g	150	154
Kapgarde	Hammersly Lake	10	g		155
Kapgarde	Kaki De La Pree	11	g		135
Kapgarde	Speredek	7	g	147	154
Kapgarde	Style De Garde	4	g	137	
Kapgarde	Ubak	10	g	146	
Kapgarde	Ultragold	10	g		142
Kayf Tara	*A Great View*	*7*	*g*	*131*	*121*
Kayf Tara	A Little Magic	7	g		140
Kayf Tara	Ballyandy	7	g		140
Kayf Tara	Ballybolley	9	g		147
Kayf Tara	Bells Of Ailsworth	8	g		132
Kayf Tara	Blaklion	9	g		161
Kayf Tara	Brother Tedd	9	g		137

				Official Ratings as of Jan 2018	
Sire	***Horse***	***Age***	***Sex***	***Hurdles***	***Chase***
Kayf Tara	Bucking The Trend	10	g	128	130
Kayf Tara	Carole's Destrier	10	g		146
Kayf Tara	Champagne At Tara	9	g		132
Kayf Tara	Copper Kay	8	m	132	132
Kayf Tara	*Edwulf*	*9*	*g*		*152*
Kayf Tara	Final Nudge	9	g		144
Kayf Tara	Flintham	9	g		133
Kayf Tara	*Glenloe*	*7*	*g*	*134*	
Kayf Tara	*Good Thyne Tara*	*8*	*m*	*134*	
Kayf Tara	*Identity Thief*	*8*	*g*	*153*	
Kayf Tara	Just Cameron	11	g		145
Kayf Tara	Kayf Adventure	7	g		139
Kayf Tara	Kayf Grace	8	m	140	
Kayf Tara	*Lieutenant Colonel*	*9*	*g*	*141*	*137*
Kayf Tara	*Moyross*	*7*	*g*	*133*	
Kayf Tara	No Comment	7	g	145	145
Kayf Tara	North Hill Harvey	7	g		152
Kayf Tara	Poppy Kay	8	m	137	
Kayf Tara	Potters Story	6	g	133	
Kayf Tara	Premier Bond	8	g	135	139
Kayf Tara	Relentless Dreamer	9	g		138
Kayf Tara	Rons Dream	8	m	137	132
Kayf Tara	Secret Investor	6	g	135	
Kayf Tara	Silver Kayf	6	g	132	
Kayf Tara	*Special Tiara*	*11*	*g*		*163*
Kayf Tara	Tara View	7	m	130	
Kayf Tara	Tea For Two	9	g		164
Kayf Tara	Thistlecrack	10	g	167	167
Kayf Tara	Value At Risk	9	g	145	132
Kayf Tara	War Sound	9	g		130
Kayf Tara	Yalltari	7	g	130	
King's Theatre	Acting Lass	7	g		149
King's Theatre	As I See It	6	g	130	
King's Theatre	Ballycross	7	g		131
King's Theatre	*Bellshill*	*8*	*g*		*150*
King's Theatre	Born Survivor	7	g		141
King's Theatre	Briery Belle	9	m		137
King's Theatre	Briery Queen	9	m		142
King's Theatre	*Carlingford Lough*	*12*	*g*		*152*
King's Theatre	Cogry	9	g		138
King's Theatre	Cue Card	12	g		166
King's Theatre	*Diamond King*	*10*	*g*		*145*
King's Theatre	Double Treasure	7	g		150
King's Theatre	*Fine Theatre*	*8*	*g*	*122*	*133*
King's Theatre	For Good Measure	7	g		135
King's Theatre	Happy Diva	7	m	135	128
King's Theatre	Jacks Last Hope	9	g	147	139
King's Theatre	Junction Fourteen	9	g		138
King's Theatre	*Killiney Court*	*9*	*g*	*111*	*131*
King's Theatre	King Of Realms	6	g	133	

				Official Ratings as of Jan 2018	
Sire	***Horse***	***Age***	***Sex***	***Hurdles***	***Chase***
King's Theatre	King's Odyssey	9	g		139
King's Theatre	Kingswell Theatre	9	g		142
King's Theatre	L'Ami Serge	8	g	159	154
King's Theatre	*Logical Song*	*9*	*g*	*115*	*135*
King's Theatre	Master Dee	9	g		145
King's Theatre	Minella Aris	7	g		137
King's Theatre	*Minella Awards*	*7*	*g*	*142*	
King's Theatre	Minella Charmer	7	g	132	
King's Theatre	Minellacelebration	8	g		133
King's Theatre	Morello Royale	8	m	135	125
King's Theatre	Morning Royalty	11	g	130	136
King's Theatre	*Mystic Theatre*	*7*	*m*	*141*	
King's Theatre	Oh Land Abloom	8	g	133	
King's Theatre	*Peregrine Run*	*8*	*g*		*144*
King's Theatre	Pete The Feat	14	g		133
King's Theatre	Regal Encore	10	g	145	150
King's Theatre	Royal Regatta	10	g		150
King's Theatre	Royal Vacation	8	g	142	147
King's Theatre	*Shaneshill*	*9*	*g*	*155*	*157*
King's Theatre	Shuil Royale	13	g		141
King's Theatre	Southfield Theatre	10	g		139
King's Theatre	The Druids Nephew	11	g		143
King's Theatre	The Dutchman	8	g	140	148
King's Theatre	The New One	10	g	163	
King's Theatre	Theatre Guide	11	g		152
King's Theatre	Theatre Territory	8	m		132
King's Theatre	Tintern Theatre	7	g		138
King's Theatre	William Henry	8	g	151	
Martaline	Agrapart	7	g	161	
Martaline	*Carter Mckay*	*7*	*g*	*138*	
Martaline	Demon D'Aunou	5	g	130	
Martaline	Diese Des Bieffes	5	g	137	
Martaline	*Disko*	*7*	*g*		*164*
Martaline	*Karalee*	*7*	*m*	*138*	
Martaline	Malaya	4	m	134	
Martaline	Marracudja	7	g		140
Martaline	*Mon Lino*	*6*	*g*	*132*	
Martaline	Ramses De Teillee	6	g		148
Martaline	Snow Leopardess	6	m	135	
Martaline	*Squouateur*	*7*	*g*		*135*
Martaline	Terrefort	5	g		151
Martaline	Theligny	7	g	137	
Martaline	*Ucello Conti*	*10*	*g*		*147*
Martaline	Viconte Du Noyer	9	g		147
Martaline	We Have A Dream	4	g	145	
Midnight Legend	Aye Aye Charlie	6	g	134	
Midnight Legend	Clan Legend	8	g	127	132
Midnight Legend	Cresswell Breeze	8	m		137
Midnight Legend	Cresswell Legend	7	g	131	
Midnight Legend	Crosspark	8	g		134

				Official Ratings as of Jan 2018	
Sire	**Horse**	**Age**	**Sex**	**Hurdles**	**Chase**
Midnight Legend	Dusky Legend	8	m	139	139
Midnight Legend	Graceful Legend	7	m	136	
Midnight Legend	Jameson	6	g		140
Midnight Legend	Mercian Prince	7	g		141
Midnight Legend	Midnight Cowboy	7	g		137
Midnight Legend	Midnight Jazz	8	m	136	
Midnight Legend	Midnight Shadow	5	g	134	
Midnight Legend	Midnight Shot	8	g		140
Midnight Legend	Midnight Tour	8	m	146	
Midnight Legend	Midnight Tune	7	m	130	
Midnight Legend	Miss Crick	7	m	132	127
Midnight Legend	Monbeg Legend	8	g	133	
Midnight Legend	Potters Legend	8	g		130
Midnight Legend	Quite By Chance	9	g		145
Midnight Legend	Seeyouatmidnight	10	g	149	154
Midnight Legend	Shades Of Midnight	8	g		135
Midnight Legend	Sir Ivan	8	g		139
Midnight Legend	*Sizing John*	*8*	*g*		*170*
Midnight Legend	Warriors Tale	9	g		149
Midnight Legend	Whataknight	9	g	138	
Midnight Legend	William H Bonney	7	g	134	
Milan	Anteros	10	g	132	112
Milan	*Apache Stronghold*	*10*	*g*		*141*
Milan	Barel Of Laughs	12	g		138
Milan	Beat That	10	g	147	142
Milan	Big River	8	g		140
Milan	Brillare Momento	7	m	135	
Milan	*Castello Sforza*	*7*	*g*	*133*	
Milan	*Davids Charm*	*7*	*g*	*143*	
Milan	Double Shuffle	8	g		166
Milan	El Bandit	7	g	141	141
Milan	Emerging Force	8	g		138
Milan	Forza Milan	6	g	138	
Milan	*Full Cry*	*8*	*g*		*131*
Milan	If The Cap Fits	6	g	145	
Milan	Isaacstown Lad	11	g	132	
Milan	*Jaime Sommers*	*6*	*m*	*130*	
Milan	Jessber's Dream	8	m	139	139
Milan	*Jezki*	*10*	*g*	*153*	
Milan	*Josies Orders*	*10*	*g*	*119*	*135*
Milan	Le Reve	10	g	132	139
Milan	Lord Wishes	11	g	120	133
Milan	*Mall Dini*	*8*	*g*		*143*
Milan	Max Ward	9	g		143
Milan	Milansbar	11	g		143
Milan	*Monbeg Notorious*	*7*	*g*		*150*
Milan	New To This Town	7	g	132	
Milan	Oakley Hall	6	g	130	
Milan	*Ordinary World*	*8*	*g*		*149*
Milan	*Roaring Bull*	*5*	*g*	*133*	

				Official Ratings as of Jan 2018	
Sire	***Horse***	***Age***	***Sex***	***Hurdles***	***Chase***
Milan	*Rogue Trader*	*9*	*g*		*135*
Milan	Run To Milan	6	g	134	
Milan	Santini	6	g	150	
Milan	Senor Lombardy	5	g	135	
Milan	Singlefarmpayment	8	g		145
Milan	Sizing Granite	10	g		153
Milan	*Sort It Out*	*9*	*g*	*135*	*118*
Milan	Terry The Fish	6	g	133	
Milan	Tommy Rapper	7	g	130	
Milan	Tornado In Milan	12	g	134	126
Milan	What A Moment	8	g		138
Montjeu	Eminent Poet	7	g	133	
Montjeu	Gabrial The Great	9	g	125	138
Montjeu	*Ivanovich Gorbatov*	*6*	*g*	*147*	
Montjeu	John Constable	7	g	156	
Montjeu	*Open Eagle*	*9*	*g*	*153*	
Montjeu	*Plinth*	*8*	*g*	*135*	
Montjeu	*Tigris River*	*7*	*g*	*147*	
Network	*A Sizing Network*	*8*	*8*		*133*
Network	*Acapella Bourgeois*	*8*	*g*		*150*
Network	*Ball D'Arc*	*7*	*g*		*157*
Network	*Bel Ami De Sivola*	*7*	*g*	*127*	*130*
Network	*Blazer*	*7*	*g*		*135*
Network	*Bon Papa*	*7*	*g*		*139*
Network	Catamaran Du Seuil	6	g		133
Network	Cuirassier Dempire	6	g		130
Network	Dame Rose	5	m	140	
Network	*Delta Work*	*5*	*g*	*136*	
Network	*Le Richebourg*	*5*	*g*	*141*	
Network	Saint Are	12	g	140	
Network	Virtuel D'Oudon	9	g	130	
Network	Work Du Breteau	8	g	125	137
Old Vic	Audacious Plan	9	g	127	135
Old Vic	Ballyoptic	8	g	154	150
Old Vic	Call Me Vic	11	g		134
Old Vic	*Folsom Blue*	*11*	*g*	*128*	*133*
Old Vic	Grand Vision	12	g		135
Old Vic	*Killultagh Vic*	*9*	*g*	*150*	*153*
Old Vic	Knock House	9	g	130	139
Old Vic	Southfield Vic	9	g		142
Old Vic	Village Vic	11	g		155
Oscar	*Any Second Now*	*6*	*g*		*145*
Oscar	Bags Groove	7	g	145	
Oscar	Ballycrystal	7	g	130	130
Oscar	Beer Goggles	7	g	159	
Oscar	Boyhood	7	g	139	
Oscar	Clondaw Castle	6	g	132	
Oscar	Clondaw Kaempfer	10	g	131	
Oscar	Courtown Oscar	9	g		130
Oscar	Dashing Oscar	8	g	139	

				Official Ratings as of Jan 2018	
Sire	***Horse***	***Age***	***Sex***	***Hurdles***	***Chase***
Oscar	Divine Spear	7	g		143
Oscar	*Draycott Place*	*9*	*g*	*115*	*130*
Oscar	*Drumacoo*	*9*	*g*	*128*	*135*
Oscar	Enniscoffey Oscar	6	g	142	
Oscar	Finian's Oscar	6	g	151	153
Oscar	Fortunate George	8	g		131
Oscar	God's Own	10	g		158
Oscar	Gunfleet	6	g	130	
Oscar	Kilbricken Storm	7	g	144	
Oscar	Lake View Lad	8	g		136
Oscar	*Lord Windermere*	*12*	*g*		*144*
Oscar	Louis' Vac Pouch	6	g	145	
Oscar	*Mallowney*	*12*	*g*	*131*	*144*
Oscar	Minella Awards	7	g	145	
Oscar	*Montys Meadow*	*10*	*g*	*126*	*138*
Oscar	O Maonlai	10	g		134
Oscar	*Oathkeeper*	*8*	*g*	*130*	
Oscar	O'Faolains Boy	11	g		133
Oscar	Oscar Hoof	10	g	132	132
Oscar	*Oscar Knight*	*9*	*g*	*125*	*136*
Oscar	*Oscar Sam*	*9*	*g*	*136*	
Oscar	Oscar Sunset	11	g	130	130
Oscar	*Our Duke*	*8*	*g*		*167*
Oscar	Our Kaempfer	9	g	133	140
Oscar	Ozzie The Oscar	7	g	136	142
Oscar	Paisley Park	6	g	145	
Oscar	Pobbles Bay	8	g		141
Oscar	Rather Be	7	g	143	143
Oscar	*Rightdownthemiddle*	*10*	*g*	*117*	*132*
Oscar	River Wylde	7	g	144	144
Oscar	Rock On Oscar	8	g		132
Oscar	Rocklander	9	g		142
Oscar	Sneaky Feeling	6	g	132	
Oscar	Splash Of Ginge	10	g		138
Oscar	Wilde Blue Yonder	9	g	133	
Poliglote	Casse Tete	6	g		133
Poliglote	Chirico Vallis	6	g		133
Poliglote	Golden Birthday	7	g	147	
Poliglote	*Let's Dance*	*6*	*m*	*145*	
Poliglote	Pistol Park	7	g		132
Poliglote	*Poli Roi*	*6*	*g*	*136*	
Poliglote	Politologue	7	g		165
Poliglote	*Roi Des Francs*	*9*	*g*		*149*
Poliglote	Top Notch	7	g		164
Poliglote	Wonderful Charm	10	g		138
Presenting	Arthur's Gift	7	g	135	
Presenting	*Ballycasey*	*11*	*g*		*157*
Presenting	Ballykan	8	g		133
Presenting	Ballymalin	8	g		132
Presenting	*Ballyoisin*	*7*	*g*		*156*

				Official Ratings as of Jan 2018	
Sire	Horse	Age	Sex	Hurdles	Chase
Presenting	Braavos	7	g	134	130
Presenting	*Brelade*	*6*	*g*	*140*	*139*
Presenting	Bright New Dawn	11	g		140
Presenting	Chef D'Equipe	6	g		132
Presenting	*Childrens List*	*8*	*g*		*145*
Presenting	Dadsintrouble	8	g		133
Presenting	Doing Fine	10	g	132	136
Presenting	*Dromnea*	*11*	*g*		*133*
Presenting	Drumcliff	7	g		141
Presenting	Duel At Dawn	8	g		141
Presenting	Duke Of Navan	10	g		145
Presenting	Dunraven Storm	13	g		132
Presenting	El Presente	5	g	130	
Presenting	Festive Affair	10	g		135
Presenting	Give Me A Copper	8	g	146	146
Presenting	Gold Present	8	g		155
Presenting	Goodtoknow	10	g		133
Presenting	*Haymount*	*9*	*g*		*145*
Presenting	I'dliketheoption	7	g		131
Presenting	*Lord Scoundrel*	*9*	*g*		*151*
Presenting	Lough Derg Farmer	6	g	132	132
Presenting	Minella Present	9	g	134	
Presenting	Mount Mews	7	g	142	140
Presenting	Movewiththetimes	7	g		142
Presenting	*Mr Diablo*	*9*	*g*		*138*
Presenting	Pair Of Jacks	10	g		135
Presenting	*Pleasant Company*	*10*	*g*		*145*
Presenting	Present Man	8	g	140	149
Presenting	Reigning Supreme	7	g	134	134
Presenting	Rene's Girl	8	m		144
Presenting	Resolution Bay	6	g		130
Presenting	*Rogue Angel*	*10*	*g*		*131*
Presenting	Slate House	6	g	143	
Presenting	*Snow Falcon*	*8*	*g*		*150*
Presenting	Some Invitation	7	g	138	
Presenting	Sonneofpresenting	8	g		135
Presenting	Southfield Royale	8	g	128	133
Presenting	*Stellar Notion*	*10*	*g*		*138*
Presenting	Sugar Baron	8	g		137
Presenting	Theo's Charm	8	g	137	132
Presenting	*Three Wise Men*	*8*	*g*		*135*
Presenting	*Thunder And Roses*	*10*	*g*		*141*
Presenting	Top Gamble	10	g		152
Presenting	Toviere	7	g		132
Presenting	*Yorkhill*	*8*	*g*	*156*	*164*
Robin Des Champs	*Blow By Blow*	*7*	*g*	*132*	
Robin Des Champs	Champers On Ice	8	g	140	
Robin Des Champs	Delegate	8	g		134
Robin Des Champs	Duke Des Champs	8	g		135
Robin Des Champs	Geordie Des Champs	7	g		137

				Official Ratings as of Jan 2018	
Sire	***Horse***	***Age***	***Sex***	***Hurdles***	***Chase***
Robin Des Champs	Hell's Kitchen	7	g		145
Robin Des Champs	Ice Cool Champs	7	g	133	133
Robin Des Champs	*Listen Dear*	*8*	*m*		*140*
Robin Des Champs	Noble Robin	7	g	130	
Robin Des Champs	Pearl Royale	6	m		137
Robin Des Champs	*Potters Point*	*8*	*g*		*148*
Robin Des Champs	Robbin'hannon	7	g	138	133
Robin Des Champs	Robinshill	7	g		142
Robin Des Champs	Sizing Tennessee	10	g		145
Robin Des Champs	Tales Of The Tweed	6	g	134	
Robin Des Champs	*Tombstone*	*8*	*g*		*147*
Robin Des Champs	Way Back Then	7	g	135	
Robin Des Champs	*Woodland Opera*	*8*	*g*		*148*
Saddler Maker	*Alpha Des Obeaux*	*8*	*g*	*151*	*156*
Saddler Maker	*Apple's Jade*	*6*	*m*	*157*	
Saddler Maker	Apple's Shakira	4	m	146	
Saddler Maker	Bouvreuil	7	g		142
Saddler Maker	Bristol De Mai	7	g		165
Saddler Maker	Cepage	6	g		140
Saddler Maker	Chef Des Obeaux	6	g	145	
Saddler Maker	*Dinaria Des Obeaux*	*5*	*m*		*139*
Saddler Maker	*Discorama*	*5*	*g*	*136*	
Saddler Maker	Label Des Obeaux	7	g		149
Saint Des Saints	Aintree My Dream	8	g		136
Saint Des Saints	*Burrows Saint*	*5*	*g*	*133*	
Saint Des Saints	Connetable	6	g	135	
Saint Des Saints	Days Of Heaven	8	g		149
Saint Des Saints	*Djakadam*	*9*	*g*		*165*
Saint Des Saints	*Fabulous Saga*	*6*	*g*	*145*	
Saint Des Saints	Le Rocher	8	g		144
Saint Des Saints	Melrose Boy	6	g	135	
Saint Des Saints	Romain De Senam	6	g		142
Saint Des Saints	Saint Calvados	5	g		154
Saint Des Saints	Sainte Ladylime	7	m	135	132
Saint Des Saints	Sametegal	9	g		143
Saint Des Saints	Wait For Me	8	g	142	139
Shantou	*Airlie Beach*	*8*	*m*	*144*	
Shantou	Ballynagour	12	g		138
Shantou	Battle Of Shiloh	9	g		137
Shantou	Beware The Bear	8	g		150
Shantou	Bun Doran	7	g		139
Shantou	*Death Duty*	*7*	*g*		*157*
Shantou	*Jimmy Two Times*	*9*	*g*	*132*	*130*
Shantou	*Shantou Bob*	*10*	*g*	*145*	
Shantou	Shantou Bob	10	g	147	
Shantou	Shantou Flyer	8	g		153
Shantou	Shantou Rock	6	g		148
Shantou	Shantou Village	8	g		148
Shantou	Smaoineamh Alainn	6	m	137	
Shantou	Taj Badalandabad	8	g	138	

				Official Ratings as of Jan 2018	
Sire	**Horse**	**Age**	**Sex**	**Hurdles**	**Chase**
Shantou	*Tellthemnuttin*	*7*	*m*	*132*	
Shantou	The Mighty Don	6	g	132	
Shantou	*The Storyteller*	*7*	*g*	*142*	*147*
Shantou	The Tourard Man	12	g	148	
Shantou	*Tully East*	*8*	*g*	*138*	*144*
Shantou	*Wounded Warrior*	*9*	*g*		*136*
Shirocco	Art Of Payroll	9	g	137	142
Shirocco	Casablanca Mix	6	m	138	138
Shirocco	*Minella Rocco*	*8*	*g*		*161*
Shirocco	Minella Rocco	8	g		162
Shirocco	Rock The Kasbah	8	g		149
Sinndar	Night Of Sin	5	g	131	
Sinndar	*Noble Inn*	*8*	*g*	*132*	
Sinndar	Project Bluebook	5	g	141	
Stowaway	Ballydine	8	g		131
Stowaway	*Champagne Harmony*	*8*	*g*		*134*
Stowaway	*Dicey O'Reilly*	*6*	*g*	*131*	
Stowaway	*Gun Digger*	*6*	*g*	*131*	
Stowaway	Highway One O One	6	g	133	
Stowaway	*Mind's Eye*	*6*	*g*	*133*	
Stowaway	*Monkshood*	*6*	*g*	*136*	
Stowaway	*On Fiddlers Green*	*8*	*g*		*133*
Stowaway	On The Blind Side	6	g	153	
Stowaway	*Outlander*	*10*	*g*		*163*
Stowaway	*Paloma Blue*	*6*	*g*	*135*	
Stowaway	Stowaway Magic	7	g	140	140
Stowaway	The Worlds End	7	g	152	
Stowaway	*Trainwreck*	*6*	*g*	*136*	
Stowaway	Tree Of Liberty	6	g		138
Stowaway	*Us And Them*	*5*	*g*	*136*	
Turgeon	Alcala	8	g		150
Turgeon	*Sandsend*	*5*	*g*	*142*	
Vinnie Roe	Barney Dwan	8	g		145
Vinnie Roe	Bigbadjohn	9	g		133
Vinnie Roe	Bob Ford	11	g		130
Vinnie Roe	Cut The Corner	10	g	123	133
Vinnie Roe	De Dollar Man	7	g		139
Vinnie Roe	*De Name Escapes Me*	*8*	*g*	*130*	*119*
Vinnie Roe	Irish Roe	7	m	145	
Vinnie Roe	*The Crafty Butcher*	*11*	*g*	*127*	*135*
Vinnie Roe	Vinndication	5	g	141	
Vinnie Roe	Vinnie Lewis	7	g		136
Vinnie Roe	Vintage Vinnie	9	g		141
Vinnie Roe	Young Dillon	9	g	133	125
Voix Du Nord	Aristo Du Plessis	8	g	138	
Voix Du Nord	*Bachasson*	*7*	*g*		*160*
Voix Du Nord	Defi Du Seuil	5	g	157	
Voix Du Nord	Destrier	5	g	130	
Voix Du Nord	*Duca De Thaix*	*5*	*g*	*136*	
Voix Du Nord	*Espoir D'Allen*	*4*	*g*	*144*	

				Official Ratings as of Jan 2018	
Sire	**Horse**	**Age**	**Sex**	**Hurdles**	**Chase**
Voix Du Nord	*Val De Ferbet*	*9*	*g*	*134*	*148*
Voix Du Nord	Vaniteux	9	g		151
Voix Du Nord	Vibrato Valtat	9	g		147
Voix Du Nord	*Vieux Morvan*	*9*	*g*	*128*	*133*
Voix Du Nord	Voix D'Eau	8	g		141
Voix Du Nord	*Voix Du Reve*	*6*	*g*	*144*	
Voix Du Nord	*Vroum Vroum Mag*	*9*	*m*	*152*	*153*
Westerner	*Beyond The Law*	*6*	*g*	*137*	
Westerner	*Champagne West*	*10*	*g*		*157*
Westerner	Cole Harden	9	g		134
Westerner	Crucial Role	6	g	137	
Westerner	*Dont Tell No One*	*10*	*g*		*134*
Westerner	Eamon An Cnoic	7	g		133
Westerner	*Empire Of Dirt*	*11*	*g*		*162*
Westerner	Fly Camp	8	g	132	
Westerner	Hello George	9	g	135	
Westerner	*Hurricane Darwin*	*8*	*g*	*127*	*132*
Westerner	I Shot The Sheriff	11	g	132	
Westerner	Kansas City Chief	9	g	134	
Westerner	Keeper Hill	7	g		143
Westerner	Kilfinichen Bay	10	g	130	132
Westerner	Lisdoonvarna Lad	6	g	132	
Westerner	Lough Derg Spirit	6	g	138	
Westerner	Overland Flyer	7	g	139	
Westerner	Report To Base	6	g		130
Westerner	Rocky's Treasure	7	g	134	
Westerner	Skipthecuddles	7	g	130	
Westerner	Slanelough	6	g	130	
Westerner	Theo	8	g		130
Westerner	*Three Stars*	*8*	*g*		*137*
Westerner	*Total Recall*	*9*	*g*	*125*	*156*
Westerner	*Velocity Boy*	*9*	*g*		*133*
Westerner	Wakanda	9	g		148
Westerner	West Approach	8	g		148
Westerner	Westend Story	7	g	134	
Westerner	Western Climate	9	g	132	137
Westerner	Western Miller	7	g		141
Westerner	Western Ryder	6	g	146	
Westerner	*Westerner Point*	*9*	*g*	*117*	*134*
Westerner	*Westerners Son*	*10*	*g*	*113*	*130*
Westerner	Wild West Wind	9	g		144
Westerner	Work In Progress	8	g		138
Winged Love	Baywing	9	g		142
Winged Love	*Bless The Wings*	*13*	*g*		*137*
Winged Love	Coeur Blimey	7	g	132	
Winged Love	Firebird Flyer	11	g	118	130
Winged Love	Fletchers Flyer	10	g		137
Winged Love	*Joey Sasa*	*9*	*g*	*138*	
Winged Love	Josses Hill	10	g		150
Winged Love	Knight Of Noir	9	g	147	142

				Official Ratings as of Jan 2018	
Sire	***Horse***	***Age***	***Sex***	***Hurdles***	***Chase***
Winged Love	Lovenormoney	7	g	137	
Winged Love	Perfect Candidate	11	g		154
Winged Love	Rock Gone	10	g		136
Winged Love	*Some Plan*	*10*	*g*		*143*
Winged Love	Spookydooky	10	g		130
Winged Love	Treackle Tart	6	m	135	

Published by James Iddiols
Printed by Penrose Group

UK £12.95